The Antelope

The Antelope

The Ordeal of the Recaptured Africans in the Administrations of James Monroe and John Quincy Adams

John T. Noonan, Jr.

University of California Press

Berkeley · Los Angeles · London

University of California Press
Berkeley and Los Angeles, California
University of California Press, Ltd. London, England

ISBN 0-520-03319-1
Library of Congress Catalog Card Number: 76-2888
Printed in the United States of America

Contents

Acknowledgments

I am indebted to Gerald T. Dunne, Joe Feldman, Gerald Gunther, Paul Sniderman, Kenneth Stampp, and to my father, John T. Noonan, and my wife, Mary Lee, for reading the manuscript and making valuable criticisms. I know no keener or more generous critics. The first draft was written at the Center for Advanced Studies in the Behavioral Sciences. I know no more congenial place to work.

Berkeley, August 15, 1976 John T. Noonan, Jr.

· 1 ·

The Very Sensitive Agent

At the end of June 1820, in the last year of the first term of President James Monroe, a ship flying the revolutionary flag of José Artigas was boarded by a Treasury revenue cutter off the northern coast of Florida and discovered to have on board about 280 human beings in chains. The conduct of the slave trade was a federal crime, and it was reasonably inferred that the ship, the *Antelope,* was criminally conveying the natives of Africa for sale in a Southern market. For the next eight years they were to be the object of attention by President Monroe himself, and his successor as President, John Quincy Adams, Attorney General William Wirt, two Secretaries of the Navy, the Monroe Cabinet as a whole, the Supreme Court of the United States headed by John Marshall, both branches of Congress, a variety of other administrators, officers and judges, and the American Colonization Society.

As the attention given the Africans by any of these persons or institutions was sporadic, they have been, for the most part, ignored by the biographers of the men of the Silver Age of the American Republic and neglected by the historians of the three branches of American government. If mentioned at all, it is as part of a lawsuit, the case of *The Antelope,* where their status as merchandise was asserted by representatives of Spain and Portugal. Their names go unrecorded. Although their role was to suffer while their lawyers, Richard Wylly Habersham, William Wirt and Francis Scott Key, acted for them and other lawyers acted against them, they are part of a story which touches the official conduct of Monroe, Adams, Marshall and their colleagues and the workings of the institutions they served. The story begins in Washington.

The Department of State. October 1818

At two in the afternoon of October 17, 1818, Abbé José Francisco Correia, Minister of Portugal to the United States, called at the office of John Quincy Adams, Secretary of State of the United States. Abbé Correia was one of the few men in the capital of whom Adams entertained a high opinion. A scientist who had co-founded the Royal Academy of Science in Lisbon, a botanist who had first classified the plants of North America on the Linnaean system, the Abbé had moved as a student of nature into Jefferson's circle, and through Jefferson had become the friend of Madison and Monroe. He was equally welcome as a scholar with Adams. But he was no pedant. He was, in Adams' words, "a man of extensive and general literature," "of brilliant wit," and "so much of a philosopher as to have incurred the vindictive pursuit of the Inquisition." He was "insinuating and fascinating in his manners and deportment." Sixty-eight years of age, he was "as lively as if he were but twenty-five." He was the official representative of the King of Portugal to the government of the United States, but he was a diplomat whose diplomacy consisted "principally in affecting to be anything but a diplomat." He came to visit the Secretary of State "as a familiar acquaintance, to talk literature and philosophy, as a domestic inmate, to gossip over a cup of tea."

John Quincy Adams was a statesman with twenty years of experience in the courts of Prussia, Russia and Great Britain. He had negotiated the end of the War of 1812, where America lost the war and won the peace. He was soon, in 1819-20, to negotiate the peaceful severance of all Florida from Spain. He was in 1823 to draft the foundation of Western Hemisphere independence, the Monroe Doctrine. No innocent, the acutest mind in the Administration, he did not seem a man to be gulled by a dozen Abbé Correias. Yet he was charmed by him, fascinated by him, listened to him and did not suspect that Correia spoke other than as a patriotic Portuguese.

President Monroe had a slightly different view of the Abbé. The President was the third of the three great Virginian friends whom the Abbé half-genially, half-mockingly, and not to their faces, called "the Presidential Trinity." The Abbé had become his very good friend when Monroe was Madison's Secretary of State, and the Abbé, the first year on his post, had engineered a brilliant legislative victory. The Minister of Portugal had taken the lead in persuading Congress to amend the Neutrality Act. To achieve this result, the Abbé had needed Secretary of State Monroe's cooperation and the blessing of the Speaker of the House, Henry Clay; and so well had he done as a novice lobbyist that a potentially controversial change had passed the Congress almost without debate. The impact of the measure had been to injure the colonies of Spain in revolt against their mother country. As amended, the Neutrality Act made it a federal crime to prepare Latin American privateers in ports of the United States. North American participation in privateering against Spain became officially forbidden. The most interesting aspect of Abbé Correia's triumph was why he had worked so hard to secure it. Portugal in 1815 was at peace. It took a farsighted diplomat to guess that Portugal would need the protection of the Neutrality Act too; and few diplomats are known not only to foresee the future but to act decisively to anticipate it. When Correia lobbied, a nation other than his own had been the apparent gainer. The Abbé had been — to quote Monroe himself — "not only the very sensitive and useful agent of Portugal but the benefactor of Spain." It was this breadth of service, this duality of masters or beneficiaries, which President Monroe recalled and pondered three years later when the Abbé Correia in person broke in upon the President's deliberations on the fate of the *Antelope.*

On October 17, 1818, Abbé Correia had never heard of the *Antelope,* but he was making his first move to engage the mind of the Secretary of State on the question of the plunderers of Portuguese property who sailed from North American havens. Portugal was now at war, and the threat to commerce under the flag of Portugal was already visible. In Maryland, on the Patuxent, Correia told Adams, a privateer was being prepared to cruise against Portuguese shipping. The ship's captain had a commission from José Artigas. The commission from Artigas, Correia suggested, was like a commission to attack United States shipping from the Seminole Indians.

The Abbé's reference to José Artigas was to the man now known by Uruguayans as "the Father of His Country," whose statue in the shape of a *gaucho* leader today even resides in the recesses of the Smithsonian Institution, and who in 1818 was Chief of the Easterners, or the Protector of the Free Peoples of the Eastern Bank. He was at war with Spain, against whose rule he had revolted; with Buenos Aires, whose own revolutionary government he refused to acknowledge; and with Portugal, whose opportunistic effort to annex Montevideo and the Banda Oriental, or Eastern Bank of the Rió de la Plata, he opposed. The Portuguese at the moment held Montevideo, and he had neither navy nor seaport. It was the incongruity of this landlocked guerilla's commissioning a fleet on which the Abbé touched with his simile of the Seminoles.

Coming to the point of his visit, Correia asked Adams if the Neutrality Act did not authorize the President to seize the ship now in the Patuxent. Adams agreed it did, but he observed that the President could not take the facts for granted even when they were stated by his agreeable friend. The ship and her suppliers would have to be tried in the federal courts. At the mention of the judicial process, Correia became restless. A note of prudence or cynicism entered his conversation. He had no confidence, he said candidly, in the integrity of the courts of the United States. Adams did not choose to convince the Abbé that his distrust was unfounded.

The White House, Washington. November 1818

Three weeks later, November 7, President Monroe met with his Cabinet to discuss the position of the government on the American accomplices of Artigas. In Baltimore the District Attorney was prepared to prosecute several distinguished citizens of Maryland. The day before the Cabinet meeting, William Wirt, the Attorney General of the United States, had instructed him in detail how to try the captain and the crew of *The Fourth of July,* commissioned by Artigas and outfitted in violation of the Neutrality Act.

That Wirt should have instructed the District Attorney at all was remarkable in the light of the Attorney General's powers, his own view of his powers, and his subsequent report on the prospects in the case to the President. Operating without a staff at his command, the Attorney General had no supervisory authority over the federal attorneys in each state. As he was to put it himself, the law creating his office gave him a single duty as to rendering advice — to answer "questions of law propounded by *the President and Heads of Departments.*" To those limits, he affirmed in 1821, he had always confined himself "on the ground that in a government purely of laws no officer should be permitted to stretch his authority and carry the influence of his office beyond the circle which the positive law of the land has drawn about him." There was, in addition, the practical objection that without assistants, the Attorney General could not possibly advise personally all the district attorneys, and so he was "very unwilling," even in a single instance, "to create a precedent which shall encumber this burdensome office with duties foreign to it, and which seem to me to surpass the powers of any human being to perform." If, on November 6, 1818, he stretched his statutory authority, created a precedent he later forgot, and advised on the prosecution in Baltimore, Wirt scarcely did so out of any conviction that citizens of Maryland had outrageously flouted the law or out of any special zeal for their punishment.

At the Cabinet meeting, in fact, he took a negative view of the District Attorney's chances in Baltimore and seems not even to have mentioned that he had sent him detailed instructions the day before. In his opinion, Wirt told the Cabinet, the prosecution was likely to fail. The President indicated that Wirt should not identify the Administration too closely with it by going to Baltimore himself; Wirt agreed. He added in a burst of candor, successful in forestalling all questioning, that Abbé Correia had taken a lively interest in the matter. The Abbé was "pushing for the conviction of those persons very indiscreetly." He had even offered the Attorney General a fee to engage in the prosecution.

John Quincy Adams, who noted in his Diary this report by Wirt to the Cabinet, did not record whether anyone asked the Attorney General if he had accepted the fee. Knowing Wirt, Adams had a good idea of what the answer would have been. Knowing the answer, he could have inferred why Wirt had found that neither the limits of his authority nor the superhuman demands of his job had prevented him from instructing the District Attorney on November 6. But Adams did not know the instructions Wirt had given, and he did not dwell on the propriety of the Abbé's intervention.

The Courthouse, Baltimore. November 1818

"[I] am directed by the President," Adams wrote the Abbé on the 14th, "to inform you that the Attorney General is already in

Baltimore, engaged in support of the prosecutions which have been found by the grand jury there." Even in this formal communication a sense of exhilaration crept in. What greater pleasure could Adams feel than in reporting that his view of American neutrality had won out and that his friend's earnest plea for presidential action had been heeded? In his Diary, Adams did not conceal his sense of triumph. The President had been reluctant to authorize involvement by the Attorney General. The Cabinet meeting of November 7 had ended with Wirt's acquiescence in nonaction. Now, a week later, he was in Baltimore. The prestige of the Attorney General and the Administration was committed. It was due to himself, Adams told his great confidant, his Diary, that matters had so turned out. He, Adams, had "prevailed upon the President."

Adams did not ask why the Attorney General had been so agreeable to this abrupt change of policy. He did observe later that Wirt had treated his service as beyond his official duties, so he had charged the United States $1500 extra compensation for his work in Baltimore. He found no occasion to consider whether Abbé Correia had also paid for his time.

"I have been engaged by the Portuguese consul," Wirt was meantime writing his wife, "to effect the restitution of the ship to the original owners — only $500 certain — a large contingent — the certain fee nevertheless, you know from the government. — Every moment the door opens looking for indictments — expecting a juryman, or the district attorney. Here they are. A long pause — it is over." He was guilty of no crime, conscious of no conflict of interest in being paid by both the government and a private party. Uxoriously, Wirt made certain that his wife knew that his trip to Baltimore had been worthwhile.

The "original owners," those anonymous but well-advised individuals who had secured his services, had not acted directly, but through "the Portuguese consul." And who would have chosen a Maryland businessman to carry the title of "Portuguese consul"? Only the Minister of Portugal to the United States could issue the necessary commission. At a distance from Abbé Correia, the Consul had to be his man. At a slightly greater distance from Abbé Correia, the Attorney General of the United States carried out a task the Abbé had paid for in part and lobbied for in whole.

Five years before, when the Abbé had arrived in the United States, he had been a refugee, reduced to running a school in Philadelphia to stay alive. When the wheel of fortune had made him Minister to the United States, it had not made him a rich man. The Portuguese Empire was not known to pay its diplomats on a princely scale. Behind Abbé Correia there had to lie nameless interests ready with cash and adroit in their selection of human agents.

The Department of State. March 1819

A year later the threat to vessels under the flag of Portugal from captains holding the commission of José Artigas had not abated. Why, Abbé Correia asked Adams, could they not all be declared pirates and so subject to that ultimate sanction, the death penalty? What was wanted was new legislation; for the existing law on piracy (robbery committed by "any person" on the high seas) had been gutted by Chief Justice Marshall's interpretation the year before. "Any person," he had held, did not mean a person who was on a ship "belonging exclusively to subjects of a foreign state" and who exclusively robbed "persons within a vessel belonging exclusively to subjects of a foreign state." Adams viewed Marshall's decision as "a sample of judicial logic — disingenuous, false, and hollow — a logic so abhorrent to my nature that it gave me an early disgust of the practice of law, and led me to an unalterable determination never to accept judicial office." It was revolting to his mind that "any person" should mean "some persons" and not "all persons." It was with a consciousness of the stupidity of the law that Adams heard the Abbé's complaint.

To illustrate the absurdity of the present situation, Abbé Correia varied his simile. What would Adams have thought during the War of 1812 if American ships had been ravaged by privateers bearing the commission of Tecumseh? The analogy between the seaportless Shawnee and the Uruguayan guerilla sank in. Committed to Correia's perspective by his friendship, by his flattery, and by having acted to help him in 1818, and convinced of the correctness of his complaint, Adams pondered how to stop the privateers. To his Diary he confided his awareness of the obstacles. Incompetence, sympathy for the Latin American revolutions, and corruption characterized the revenue inspectors and the District Attorney for Maryland. Houston, the District Judge, and Duvall, the Circuit Judge, were "feeble, inefficient men." Over them, William Pinckney, "employed by all the pirates as their counsel," domineered "like a slave-driver over his negroes." Adams' view of the federal judiciary in Maryland was not so different from the Abbé's assessment.

On March 29, ten days after the Abbé's call, Adams was visited by Hyde de Neuville, the Minister of France. The Abbé had not been acting without support at home. The government of Portugal had presented "an exceedingly energetic memorial" on the Baltimore pirates to the five great European powers currently in congress at Aix-la-Chapelle. The five — Austria, France, Great Britain, Prussia and Russia — had responded by adopting a protocol rebuking the United States. The Minister of France sternly informed Adams of this condemnation.

De Neuville's démarche confirmed all Adams' fears. He hurried at once to tell the President. The Baltimore pirates had "brought the whole body of the European allies upon us in the form of remonstrances." Portugal was truly and rightly angry at America's failure to enforce neutrality. The major Atlantic powers, England and France, stood at her side. The United States must show that it was no haven for maritime marauders.

Adams' sensitivity to the side of Portugal was only strengthened by the President's response. Monroe was unperturbed by remonstrances, whether from the Abbé alone or from all the European nations. He answered Adams — and here an irrepressible note of criticism entered Adams' Diary, otherwise loyal in word and thought to his leader — by giving his Secretary of State "directions altogether general."

The President had brushed him off, or at best left him the responsibility. The federal officers in Maryland would never act. Baltimore was "as rotten as corruption can make it." Adams alone saw the peril of antagonizing Europe and the unfairness of sheltering the guerilla's ships which preyed on Portuguese shipping. "I" — Adams' declaration was to the Diary — "must take the brunt of battle upon myself, and rely upon the justice of the cause."

If Abbé Correia had never existed, if he never had drunk a cup of tea with Adams, this clear insight into the justice of the Portuguese cause might still have been the Secretary of State's. Adams' sensibilities were those of a diplomat concerned with the opinion of foreign governments and those of a New Englander appreciative of security on the high seas. But what Adams would have seen without the Abbé is speculative. In fact it had been the task of the very sensitive agent to convince Adams of the rightness of the cause. The way the case was put by Correia, Adams could not have doubted that the most legitimate concerns of Portuguese patriotism were at stake in each taking of a ship flying the colors of Portugal.

That actual Portuguese ships were being attacked could not be disputed. But that Abbé Correia might have more than one beneficiary or master might have been considered by Adams if he recalled the information he once received. The other information had come to Adams in 1817 in London, when he had been the American Minister to Great Britain.

Lord Castlereagh, the British Foreign Secretary, had then told him that the slave trade was largely conducted by slavers from the United States. Both England and America had made the trade illegal, but the barbarities of the traffic were "more atrocious than they had been before the abolition of it had been attempted." Castlereagh cited the reports of the African Institution, a society devoted to stopping the slave trade, whose expertise, if not impartiality, was substantial. The nub of Castlereagh's information, all duly noted in Adams' Diary, was that "a great number of the vessels" in the trade were outfitted in the United States. William Wilberforce told Minister Adams the same story.

Adams discounted the great foe of slavery as a species of hypocrite — one of those who, "under sanctified visors, pursue worldly objects." His cynical comment reflected his own unwillingness to become more involved. His discounting of Castlereagh was done on higher grounds of patriotism. The War of 1812 had been fought over England's claim of right to search the ships of other nations on the high seas. America had resisted this brand of piracy. Now the wily Foreign Secretary had invented a new ground to justify the British position. Castlereagh in Adams' indignant words, was merely making "a barefaced and impudent attempt" to show that search and seizure of other nations' ships was necessary; for the thrust of his information was that without such a practice the slavers of America would continue their commerce flying the flags of the countries where the trade was legal.

Before they had rebuked the privateers of Baltimore — indeed a year before — the five powers at Aix-la-Chapelle had acted on Castlereagh's initiative and annexed to a protocol the African Institution's analysis of the trade. In that annex, available to the Secretary of State even if no ambassador brought it to his tea table, three facts stood out. The traders were currently taking 50,000 Africans each year. The sinews of the trade came from "American capital." Cover was provided by the flags of Spain and Portugal.

The Department of State. August 1819

On August 18, Adams interviewed Thaddeus Bland, whom Monroe was considering for appointment as the federal District

Judge in Maryland. Adams read to Bland the testimony given before a Baltimore grand jury by one Sands, who owned a privateer outfitted in the cause of Latin American revolutionaries. Sands had sworn that Bland, under a false name, shared the ship's ownership. On hearing this, Bland told Adams that Abbé Correia, working with the Spanish Consul in Baltimore, had instigated the grand jury proceeding and that Correia had paid for Sands' perjured testimony against him.

Adams asked for proof of Bland's innocence, and Bland went off to Baltimore and returned with evidence which Adams found conclusive. "Sands' deposition," he wrote, "is false in every particular that he states respecting Bland." There was "nothing in any responsible shape against him." Yet, though he noted and must have considered the charge Bland had made against Correia, Adams refrained from concluding that Bland's vindication meant that his story about the Abbé's vicious behavior was true.

As the nomination of Bland hung fire, and Adams wavered, he was warned once more about Correia. This time his informant was General John Mason, a munitions manufacturer. The former Commissary-General of Prisoners in the War of 1812, now a supplier of both the Spanish government and the insurgents, Mason might have been thought impartial. Although he was seen more often with the rebels, he was at least in a position to get information from both sides. He told Adams flatly that Correia had "suborned witnesses to testify against Bland." To understand the Abbé, General Mason told Adams, you had to watch his work, and to do that you had to know that "he acted by other persons." To see him work, Mason observed, "you must look three or four men off from him."

Neither then nor elsewhere did Adams ever exhibit any curiosity in how Correia had sums of ready cash at his disposal to offer fees to the Attorney General and to suborn witnesses in Baltimore. It was a measure of Adams' devotion to his friend and to the justice of the Portuguese position that he, a prudent, experienced, distrustful, even cynical statesman, could record every word spoken against the Abbé and still remember him as "a familiar acquaintance," " a domestic inmate," who came "to gossip over a cup of tea." Adams recorded the conversation with General Mason, but he gave no sign of recalling it when a year later the Abbé's activities on behalf of Portugal began to affect the course of the *Antelope*.

The Port of Havana. August 1819

On the 24th of the same month in which these conversations were going on in Washington, the *Antelope* herself sailed from Havana, Cuba. She had been built in Freetown, a shipbuilding center on the northern Massachusetts coast in the area soon to become the state of Maine. She was two-masted; 69 feet, 2 inches overall, 22 feet, 9 inches in the beam; with a tonnage a little over 112 tons. It is not clear that her Freetown builders had in mind her eventual use, but it is inferable. She was constructed in 1802 just before the slave trade to South Carolina was reopened and an extraordinary boom resulted for Rhode Island slave traders who acted to bring in slaves before 1808, when the Constitution would permit Congress to ban such shipments. In 1809, with the importation of slaves federally prohibited, she was registered with the customs by George Lawton, Jr., of Newport, Rhode Island, as a vessel in foreign trade sailing from Bristol, Rhode Island. A few months later Lawton canceled her registration at Savannah, Georgia, and reported to the customs that she had been sold in a foreign port.

Eight years later she reappeared as sold by one Francis Pendergast, described as a "consignee," to Messrs. Bustamente of Cadiz, Spain, for $7,700, and as registered with the Department of Marine in Cadiz. The Department's certificate identified her as "the *Antelope* alias the *Fenix*." In August 1819, Cuesta Manzanal and Brother, Havana affiliates of Messrs. Bustamente, were licensed by the Royal Governor of Cuba to sail the *Antelope* to Africa to trade for new Negroes — that is, human beings who were not slaves of Europeans or Americans and who, when brought to the New World, were new to the market. She had a crew of twenty, one slave boy, twelve muskets and twelve pistols. By contract with Cuesta Manzanal and Brother, the captain was to be paid $200 per month (a captain of the largest warship in the American navy received $100 per month), the caulker $60, the cook $40, and the sailors $35. The contract said that the captain and crew of the slaver were "to take care of the sick as well as the Negroes with the greatest humanity."

Nothing in the charter of the *Antelope* suggested that within a year she would receive the personal attention of the President of the United States or that the fate of the new Negroes she carried would reflect the conception of American responsibility which the Secretary of State shared with the Minister of Portugal.

· 2 ·

The Suspended Tortoise

The Act in Addition. March 1819

Midday on the twelfth of March, the same month in which John Quincy Adams had resolved to bear the brunt of battle for the Portuguese in Baltimore, General John Mason, Walter Jones and Francis Scott Key called upon him at his office. Mason, the impartial munitions manufacturer, and Jones, former District Attorney in Washington, he knew well. Key was a comparative stranger. "The Star-Spangled Banner" was not yet the national anthem, and Key's name was not instantly associated with it. His reputation was that of a thirty-nine-year-old Washington lawyer with a busy but local practice. To Adams he was merely "Mr. Key" or "Francis S. Key;" in later years when he came more closely to focus on him, he became "the pious informer Frank Key." His religiosity joined to political convictions different from Adams' were obvious irritants. But now in 1819 he was an unknown. As Key correctly divined, Adams viewed him as "a Cypher" or zero.

Mason, Jones and Key came to Adams on a mission. They were the Managers, or active directors, of the American Society for Colonizing the Free People of Color of the United States, better known as "The Colonization Society." The aim of the

Society was grand and simple — to establish in Africa an American colony "nourished by the resources, as well as countenanced by the authority of the Federal Government." To this haven would be transported the free blacks of the United States. Mason, Jones and Key came to secure the cooperation of the Secretary of State in this enterprise.

The Colonization Society was no abolitionist conspiracy. Abolition, the absolutist goal of wiping out the infamy of American slavery altogether, was the object of no public man in 1819. The Managers still took pains to explain that the Society "had no design to invade the rights of private property secured by the constitution and laws of the several slaveholding states and to proclaim universal emancipation!" Then for whom would the colony exist? It would be for such "free people of color as may choose to avail themselves of such asylum" and for "such slaves as their masters may be willing to emancipate." In the distant horizon a final solution of the problem of slavery in America might be glimpsed by the Society's organizers. In the end, if their scheme worked, every owner might see the beauty of liberating his slaves and returning them to Africa. But the Society did not insist upon Utopia now. Gradualists, men of Christianity, moderation and reason, the founders sought to solve the great problem of the nation by making a beginning and affording an example that would lead the way to voluntary emancipation and wholesale removal, without bloodshed, without mixing of the races, and without — it was the Society's fatal weakness — pain to the sponsors of the scheme.

The founders were from the political and legal leaders of Washington, not a class accustomed to self-sacrifice, and related to the government in such a way that their expectation of being nourished by its resources was not unreasonable. Their President was Bushrod Washington, nephew and heir of George Washington, master of Mount Vernon, and a Justice of the Supreme Court. Their Secretary, or principal executive officer, was

Elias B. Caldwell, the Clerk of the Supreme Court. First of their fourteen vice-presidents was William H. Crawford, Secretary of the Treasury. Second of the vice presidents was Henry Clay, Speaker of the House. Firmly tied to the judicial branch at its highest level, linked to the Administration and the Congress, the Society was led by members of that decent, conservative, slave-holding elite which controlled the machinery of government from 1789 to 1861.

Their first successful action, and the reason for the Managers' call on Adams, had been in Congress, where they had cured a peculiar deficiency in the previous ten years of legislation on the slave trade. Under Article II of the Constitution, Congress was denied power before January 1, 1808, to prevent "the Migration of Importation of Such Persons as any of the States now existing shall think proper to admit." The Constitution's authors deliberately did not mention slaves or slavery. In John Quincy Adams' ambivalent sexual metaphor, they had used "fig leaves under which these parts of the body politic are decently concealed." After this twenty-year period of grace for the slave traders, it became by act of Congress a crime to import slaves anywhere in the United States. It also became a federal crime to equip ships as slavers.

What Congress did not decide for ten years was what should be done with persons who were being illegally brought in as slaves when the slaver carrying them was captured. In the face of congressional silence, each state applied its own law. If illegally smuggled slaves were found in a slave state, they were auctioned by the state for its own benefit. What else, Attorney General Wirt asked rhetorically, could be done? "Should they have been turned loose as free men in the State? The impolicy of such a course is too palpable to find an advocate in anyone who is acquainted with the condition of the slave-holding States." The Attorney General did not suppose that any state would at its own expense return the slaves to their own country.

These Africans who were transported to the United States against the law, who were rescued from the criminals who had held them captive, and who nonetheless were finally made American slaves, were objects on whom the Colonization Society could exercise its benevolence. The irony of the federal government, in the course of suppressing the slave trade, becoming a supplier of slaves was evident. The society had a solution which tied together its long-run and immediate objectives and gained a base inside the government which could in time be expanded. The rescued slaves, it proposed, should be sent back to Africa. They could not be sent whence they had come, because they would only be enslaved again. They should not be cast on the shores of Africa at random. But they should be returned to their own continent, and the only way of assuring their safe reestablishment there was to establish American jurisdiction over an area to which they could be brought. The Society's plan for a colony was the only feasible response to the plight of the criminally enslaved and federally liberated Africans.

The Colonization Society turned with confidence to Congress and was not disappointed. Speaker Clay assigned its petition to a Special Committee, appointed by the Speaker. The Special Committee recommended that the suppression of the slave trade be more justly carried out by establishing a colony of the United States in Africa. The "iniquity" of federal participation in the selling of rescued slaves must be ended.

The bill the Special Committee actually drafted was more circumspect than its report. The possibly controversial term "colony" did not appear. A thrust in the direction of an African outpost could be found only by a benevolent reading. There was some debate in the House, little in the Senate, and no record vote. On March 2, 1819, "The Act in Addition to the Acts prohibiting the slave trade" was passed by Congress. In the opinion of Mason, Jones and Key, its enactment shed "a ray of light dear to humanity on the expiring moments of the Fifteenth Congress and elevated the American character in the estimation of the world."

The aim of the Society had been to avoid controversy in Congress and rely on a sympathetic Administration. The Act left every detail to the President, and what he did with the details would determine what the Act became. He was given authority to use the Navy or other armed ships wherever the slave trade was conducted and, on capture of a slaver, to take charge of the Africans aboard and assure their "safe-keeping, support, and removal beyond the United States." How the President was to safekeep and support his charges, the Act did not say. Nor did it say how he was to remove them from the United States. But it gave the President all power "to make such regulations and arrangements as he may deem expedient." The not remarkably generous sum of one hundred thousand dollars, four-tenths of one percent of the federal budget, was appropriated for the execution of the Act.

The Colonization Society at once pressed upon the Administration its interpretation of the law's open-ended phrasing. The Act did mention "agents in Africa" whom the President was given authority to appoint "to receive" the Africans he removed. If the agents were to receive Africans, they could scarcely let them starve. If the Africans were not to starve, they must labor. If they were to labor, they must have land. They could not buy the land themselves. Therefore the President must have power to acquire land in Africa. Such was the chain of inferences Mason, Jones and Key presented to Adams on March 12, nine days after President Monroe had signed the bill into law.

Before meeting with them, the Secretary of State had already given the President his views on this sudden potential expansion of the boundaries of America. It was, Adams asserted, "impossible that Congress should have had any purchase of territory in contemplation." The notion that, under the guise of more perfectly suppressing the slave trade, the United States should embark on an imperial career in Africa left the Secretary of State aghast.

Incredulous before the Colonization Society's reading of the Act, Adams was also skeptical about the motives of the Southerners who had founded the Society. Its sponsors were of four kinds: (1) "exceedingly humane weak-minded men," who honestly believed they could encourage emancipation without attacking slavery; (2) "speculators in official profits and honors, which a colonial establishment would of course produce"; (3) "speculators in political popularity"; and (4) "cunning slaveholders, who see that the plan may be carried far enough to produce the effect of raising the market price of their slaves." None of these classes, he supposed, was likely to offer him the correct construction of the Act in Addition. Partisan, prejudiced, ungenerous as Adams' analysis was, he had accurately observed conflicts within the Society which were to make its opposition to the slave trade ambiguous and its support for its African clientele erratic. Resorting to the metaphor of incongruity — that mark of lucid irony he found so congenial in Abbé Correia — Adams pronounced the Society's scheme "so far as it is sincere and honest" to be "upon a par with John Cleves Symmes' project of going to the North Pole and travelling within the nutshell of the earth." His reference was to the former Chief Justice of New Jersey, who believed the globe was hollow.

With these beliefs communicated to his Diary and with his steadfast opposition to the Colonization Society's interpretation already put before the President, Adams recorded that he received Mason, Jones and Key "with all possible civility." He told them that the purchases of Louisiana and the Oregon territory were no precedents for acquiring land outside the American continent. Much less were these territories warrant for establishing "a colonial system of government." He gave them "distinctly to understand that the late Slave-Trade Act had no reference to the settlement of a colony." In a word, he, the Secretary of State and right hand of the President, let them know that all their hopes of using the Act in Addition as a springboard for their great African dream were illusory, based on nonsense. In a final burst of metaphor, he put the insubstantiality of their case in a great imaginative sally: "To derive powers competent to this from the Slave Trade Act was an Indian cosmogony: it was mounting the world upon the elephant, and the elephant on a tortoise, with nothing for the tortoise to stand upon."

The First Test. April 1819

One o'clock, April 2, Attorney General Wirt and Secretary of the Treasury Crawford called on John Quincy Adams to consider a question Adams had raised about the meaning of the Act in Addition. Thirty to forty Africans, imported in violation of the law against the slave trade, had been discovered the year before in Georgia; they were now being advertised for sale for the benefit of the State of Georgia. When Crawford, first vice-president of the Colonization Society and its chief political patron, had heard of this, he had seized the occasion, the first offered, to put the new law into action. He had suggested to Monroe that he, the President, should assume responsibility for them and return them to Africa. The President had responded by directing Adams to take steps to achieve this end.

The President left Washington. Adams did not carry out his instructions. He called the conference with Crawford and the Attorney General instead. The Secretary of State was clear that the new law was not retroactive — Africans illegally imported before March 3, 1819, were not within its reach. The Attorney General, doubting, appeared to agree. Crawford was, so Adams put it, "finally" persuaded. He was convinced in the end by an appeal to property rights: the State of Georgia had a vested interest in the Africans which Congress had no power to divest. No one seems to have suggested that the President could simply buy the Africans from Georgia with the money so recently appropriated. Adams' victory was complete.

It was not that Adams had any love for slavery as a system.

When the great struggle over the admission of Missouri as a slave state was going on the next year in Congress, and the Administration strained to keep sectional fissures from deepening, he left a Cabinet meeting where three slaveholders, Crawford, Wirt and John Calhoun, had argued that Congress had no power to prohibit slavery in a new state. "[I]n the abstract," he observed to his Diary, "they admit that slavery is evil, they disclaim all participation in the introduction of it, and cast it all upon the shoulders of our old Grandam Britain. But when probed to the quick upon it, they show at the bottom of their souls pride and vainglory in their condition of masterdom. They fancy themselves more generous and noble-hearted than the plain freemen who labor for subsistence. They look down upon the simplicity of a Yankee's manners because he has no habits of overbearing like theirs, and cannot treat negroes like dogs." Adams did not believe that Negroes were dogs or that they should be treated other than as human beings like himself. "Oh, if but one man could arise," he exclaimed, "with a genius capable of comprehending, a heart capable of supporting, and an utterance capable of communicating those eternal truths that belong to this question, to lay bare in all its nakedness that outrage upon the goodness of God, human slavery, now is the time, and this is the occasion, upon which such a man would perform the duties of an angel upon earth!"

The passion of this passage in his Diary of February 1820 reveals Adams' perception of what he himself might be or might become. He had the genius, he might have the heart, he could speak. He was also an officer of the government of the United States and the heir apparent as its President. As long as he remained either officer or candidate, he was not likely to assume the duties of an angel.

When, a month after the Administration's decision not to aid the "thirty to forty," the Colonization Society tried to raise money from the public to buy the Africans from Georgia,

Adams declined to contribute a penny. Secretary Crawford was already his rival for the Presidency, and in his Diary, Adams observed that the Society was one of Crawford's "traps for popularity." He told the two clergymen who solicited him that the Society would do less good than evil. The Africans were sold as slaves by Georgia.

The President Persuaded. October — December 1819

"Mr. Crawford's fears are realized. The President has forgotten his promises, and what simple courtiers were we, to suppose it would be otherwise." So Key wrote in the fall of the year in which the Act in Addition had shed a ray of light on the humanity of the Fifteenth Congress. From his letter it may be inferred that, despite the opposition of the Secretary of State, the President had in the spring made a commitment to the Managers of the Colonization Society to carry out their interpretation of the Act; Monroe's initial instructions on the Georgia Negroes had indeed been evidence of his promise. Persuading the President, the Society had had the legacy of Jefferson on its side — "emancipation and deportation" was Jefferson's formula for the solution of America's race problem; and James Monroe was Jefferson's protegé and disciple. "I have always been friendly to emancipation and transportation from the country with a view to make an experiment of the practicability of the scheme," he wrote to General Mason after he was out of office. While he was in power, his friendliness to the experiment was no less, but hedged by other considerations. Now, in the fall of 1819, a new assault was necessary to "bring him back."

Key set out the strategy: "My idea is this, the President will appoint an agent, two, if he can find another (which by the by, we must do; and I wish you to look about for another), that he will send a ship of war to the coast, and probably a transport with the colored men from this country, as laborers, and some agricultural implements, and that he will authorize him to settle in our territory and make preparations for receiving the captured negroes, and I think this will do." By "our territory" Key meant land in Africa yet to be acquired by the Colonization Society. By "captured negroes," an unreflectingly ambivalent phrase he meant Africans rescued from slavers.

Key, Crawford and Caldwell, the Clerk of the Supreme Court, all worked on William Wirt to win him to the plan. Key found the Attorney General troubled chiefly by its domestic danger or "some excitement among the slaves in consequence of our proceedings." After hours of lobbying, he thought the Attorney General would be a friend. He was mistaken. On October 14, Wirt gave his official opinion. The President using the fund created by the Act in Addition was not authorized to

> 1. Appropriate any part of it to the purchase of land on the coast of Africa or elsewhere, for the purposes of a settlement.
>
> 2. Nor to the transportation of any of the free people of color in this country to Africa, nor of any other negroes or persons of color than such as are seized and captured, or ascertained by the verdict of a jury under that law to be free.
>
> 3. Nor to the purchase of carpenters' tools, etc., etc., for the purpose of making a settlement in Africa.
>
> 4. Nor to the payment of the salary and expenses of transporting an agent from this country to Africa; because the second section limits his appointment expressly to "a proper person or persons *residing* on the coast of Africa."

In his last sentence Wirt seemed to suppose that the President could only appoint residents of Africa as his agents, an interpretation almost comical in its strictness. According to the rest of the opinion, Key's idea was as dead as Symmes' expedition through the hollow earth; the tortoise was still suspended.

The importance of the plan to Crawford, and his importance to the plan, were both promptly demonstrated. He had another talk with the Attorney General. Two days after the first opinion Wirt issued a second one. Crawford's view — that is, the Society's interpretations of the law — was, he wrote, "very probably, the correct one." Still the Attorney General's conversion was not entire. He thought there was enough doubt that the President should wait until Congress had clarified his "constructive and inferential powers." But Crawford could tell Monroe that the Attorney General had acquiesced in his interpretation.

On November 10 the President indicated to Adams that he was inclined to accept Crawford's position. Adams responded that "the Act itself had evidently passed without much consideration of its purport" — a scarcely polite way of saying that the congressmen had not known what they were doing when they let the Society's bill go through — "and it would be desirable that the whole subject be reviewed by Congress." Eight months after the President had signed the law, Adams still thought the tortoise was in the air.

Crawford finally prevailed. On December 10 the President told the Cabinet of his decision, although Adams did not give up: "I objected that there was no authority given by the law to spend money to maintain the blacks in Africa at all." What would happen after the President's agents "received" them there? Were they to become instantly self-supporting? His objection was plausible, but too late. A Special Presidential Message to Congress, delivered December 19, was being drafted, informing it that the President was selecting persons in the United States to serve as his agents in Africa; if Congress thought he was wrong, it could object before he went further.

The Act, the President said in the Special Message, gave him power to deploy American armed vessels to stop the slave trade. The vessels so deployed had, as yet, made no captures. Presumably they would make captures, so he should have the agents ready to receive the Africans aboard. Otherwise, should the Africans be landed with no one to look out for them, they might perish. So far, the President followed where the Act in Addition pointed. The President supposed, the message continued, that authority to appoint agents included authority to have them provide "shelter and food and perform the other beneficent and charitable offices contemplated by the Act." So far, the logic of the President seemed irresistible.

Finally, the President said, he was acting promptly because it was "obvious that the longer these persons shall be detained in the United States in the hands of marshals, the greater would be the expense" — economy was always a strong point with James Monroe — "and for the same term would the main purpose of the law be suspended." With that accuracy of analysis which he so frequently exhibited, the President fastened on the capital consideration — the aim of the Act was to remove Africans from America; as long as they were kept in America, the Act's purpose was unachieved. No doubt he was unaware of Adams' metaphor of the suspended tortoise, confided to Adams' Diary, but in the Special Message of December 19, he could not have more flatly suppressed the objections of the Secretary of State. Committing himself in the winter to the main purpose of the Act, Monroe did not imagine how the following summer the *Antelope*, even now off the coast of Africa, would test his commitment; nor did he know that, on the very day he sent his message, a ship sailed from Baltimore whose voyage would lead to the undoing of his resolution.

A Privateer Launched. December 1819 – January 1820

On December 19, the *Columbia* sailed from Baltimore. An hermaphrodite brig painted black, with a tonnage estimated at close to two hundred tons, no head, a bowsprit without elevation, sails which were old and patched, she showed fourteen ports, carried six guns in her hold, and mounted one eighteen-pound cannon on a swivel on her deck. Simon Metcalf, her captain, carried a commission dated May 20, 1818, authorizing him to make war on the ships of Spain and Portugal and signed "José Artigas, Chief of the Easterners and Protector of the Free Peoples of the Eastern Republic."

The *Columbia,* formerly the *Baltimore,* had entered the port in the fall flying the flag of Admiral Luis Brion, commander of a force of Venezuelan revolutionaries. She had ridden empty at the wharves with only two men aboard while arrangements were made for her next mission and identity, and a crew signed on. The commissions of José Artigas came north in blank, to be filled in by Baltimorean entrepreneurs. The idea of an inexpensive entry into the slave market appealed to a Baltimorean named Mason (not, apparently, the General). The crew was recruited on the basis of shares in prizes to be taken. All of them — one Englishman, one Greek, one Welshman, and thirty or so other English-speaking sailors — went before a justice of the peace and swore that they were not American citizens.

As the *Columbia* sailed into the Chesapeake, she was boarded by a Treasury cutter, which removed four of the crew as citizens of the United States recruited in violation of the Neutrality Act. The affidavits before the justice of the peace must have been found satisfactory as to the others, some thirty-four officers and men. Abbé Correia would have smiled a cynical smile at this pro forma enforcement of federal law, capped by the cutter — ostensibly to prevent further recruitment of Americans — affording the *Columbia* an escort until she reached the Atlantic.

At sea, the *Columbia* changed her name to the *Arraganta,* and sailed for the west coast of Africa, reaching it some time in January 1820. En route, she boarded an American ship, the *Hope* of Baltimore, and took nothing; chased an English brig; fired on Portuguese forts; boarded an empty American slaver, the *Endymion,* and took nothing; attacked a ship under Spanish colors, killing one man; and boarded an empty "formerly American" slaver, flying a Spanish flag, commanded by a Mr. Wyatt from Bristol, Rhode Island. She had then been picked up by the *Myrmidon* and *Morgiana,* sloops from the British squadron patrolling for slavers. She was brought into Sierra Leone, detained for three weeks, and released with an admonition not to cruise south of the equator. As soon as she safely could, she disobeyed and headed south to the slave ports.

The *Columbia's* first strike was on a ship flying the American flag, which she found acting as a tender to a larger armed ship flying the Spanish flag, identified by a sailor aboard the *Columbia* as the *Rambler* of Bristol, Rhode Island, whom he had seen in Bristol being prepared for what people in Rhode Island called "the African trade." If the sailor was correct, the larger vessel was the property of Charles and James DeWolfe, both merchants of Bristol, the latter of whom was to be, within the year, a United States Senator from Rhode Island.

The *Rambler* was too formidable to attack, but the *Columbia* took the tender, which turned out to be the *Exchange,* a seventy-two-ton brig, also of Bristol. She had been owned by Allen Wardwell and others of that town, but had been sold and registered for foreign trade at the customs office on October 23, 1819, with William Richmond of Bristol listed as her owner and master. When raided by the *Columbia* she had on board William Richmond and at least twenty-five African persons who were being held as slaves. The *Columbia* let the Americans and their ship go, keeping the slaves.

Cabinda. March 1820

The *Antelope,* on March 23, was at anchor at Cabinda about three hundred miles below the equator on the west coast of Africa, a port under Portuguese domination and the rule of an African king. The Antelope, in the company of three ships flying the Portuguese flag, was peacefully trading with the king for the purchase of Africans.

Two weeks before, a strange ship had entered the harbor, raised the flag of a revolutionary South American republic, and menaced the unresisting *Antelope* with cannon. The stranger, as the captain of the *Antelope* later deposed, took "all he could carry off of our articles of trade," the baggage of the officers, and the sails of the ship; also "the best slaves he could select" from all the vessels. He sailed off, taking with him the cream of the *Antelope's* winter work.

With "a few slaves and a small amount of our goods" left, so the captain said, the *Antelope* remained at Cabinda. The king was still ready to do business. The unexpected attack had, from his point of view, only enlarged his market. The *Antelope* took on food and resumed the acquisition of Africans.

In the time between the raid and March 23, a number of new Africans were purchased, brought aboard and chained. More were bought and were on shore waiting shipment. Boats were ferrying them from the land to the *Antelope,* when, on the morning of the 23rd, the *Columbia* entered Cabinda, flying the flag of Spain. As she approached the *Antelope,* she raised the flag of the Banda Oriental, swung her cannon into position, and began musketry fire. She seemed, so Domingo Grondona of the *Antelope* reported, to have 120 men. With swords drawn, they boarded the *Antelope,* and without loss of life captured her crew and put them below deck with the slaves, the hatches shut and barred.

The *Columbia* took the craft showing Portuguese colors next, the largest was set on fire, the other two abandoned, and the Africans from all of them put aboard either the *Columbia* herself or the captured *Antelope.* The former crew of the *Antelope* was set ashore, and under a new captain, John Smith, the first mate of the *Columbia,* with a prize crew, and a new name — *General Ramirez,* in honor of Artigas' lieutenant, the governor of Entre Rios — she set sail in tandem with the *Columbia.*

The two ships crossed the South Atlantic to the northeast tip of Brazil. Off the coast the *Columbia* was wrecked and stranded. Captain Metcalf, part of the crew, and some of the Africans drowned or were captured by the Portuguese; no more was heard of them. The *Antelope* took aboard survivors, white and black, accommodating by the use of space on deck and the creation of tiers within the hold at least 280 Africans, probably more, in a single tiny vessel. Under Smith's command, the *Antelope* sailed north.

At Surinam, Smith offered the Africans to the Dutch for $80,000. He received a counteroffer of $50,000, rejected it, and continued north to St. Bartholomew, then a Swedish island, already the subject of a formal European protest to the government of Sweden as the seat of revolutionary privateers. Here the *Antelope* was met by Mason, whom the crew took to be the owner of the *Columbia,* as he removed a quantity of cash from the ship. The *Antelope* had none of the *Columbia's* guns and was unarmed. Mason arranged a rendezvous at sea, north of St. Bart's, where four pieces of cannon, ammunition and supplies were put aboard from another hermaphrodite under his command.

Keeping away from Cuba, the *Antelope* headed for the Hole-in-the Wall, the passage through the Caribbean islands which would lead a ship to the eastern coast of Florida. By the treaty between Spain and the United States executed February 22, 1819, Florida had been ceded by Spain. In June 1820 the treaty remained unratified, and Florida was in Spanish hands. A ship registered as Spanish and under revolutionary control could not have been brought with impunity into the jurisdiction. Once such a ship passed through the Hole-in-the-Wall, her destination had to be a market in the United States. Near the end of June 1820, the *Antelope* was off St. Augustine. She hoisted the American flag and hovered off the Florida shore at a distance of three or four miles, waiting for a signal.

· 3 ·

Safekeeping and Support by President Monroe

First Decisions. June —July 1820

At three in the afternoon of June 29, the *Antelope* was captured by the United States revenue cutter *Dallas*. The day before, the *Dallas* under the command of John Jackson had been at St. Mary's, Georgia. An informant in St. Augustine reported the appearance of a suspicious ship off the coast. Jackson proceeded to Amelia Island and took on twelve soldiers armed with muskets. Early in the morning of June 29 the *Dallas* sighted the *Antelope* between Amelia Island and the Florida coast. The *Antelope* was sailing north. The *Dallas* gave chase. The *Antelope* was overtaken in midafternoon. John Smith ordered the guns to be run out. The men, however, refused to fire on the American flag. The *Antelope* hove to and was boarded, disclosing to the boarding party an English-speaking crew and captain, the bodies of two dead Negroes and a large number of live chained Africans. The commander of the boarding party, second officer James Knight, counted 281.

Smith said that his ship was out of food and water and that he was about to put into the St. John's River for supplies. His explanation was not accepted by Jackson, who arrested him and his crew on suspicion of being engaged in the slave trade to the

United States, and brought the *Antelope* into St. Mary's with Africans still on board. Leaving the ship and the Africans there, on the Fourth of July he sailed north with his prisoners to deliver them to the nearest federal civil authorities in Savannah.

Savannah, a town of not more than 7,000 inhabitants, half of them slaves, and notorious for hospitality to privateers and slave smugglers, was also a port which the Georgia legislature had described as dangerous to aliens during "the sickly months," legislatively identified as July, August, September and October, when to bring foreigners into the area was to expose "to almost certain death the individuals whose constitutions are but illy adapted to the insalubrious climate." The state had forbidden ships to land strangers in the sickly months, and on June 29, the very day the *Antelope* was captured, Mayor Thomas U.P. Charlton had ordered the harbormaster of Savannah to be vigilant in enforcing the statute, a law calculated, he said, "to save many valuable lives."

Richard Wylly Habersham, United States District Attorney for Georgia, without directions on the point from the Administration, did not raise the question of the appropriate port for the Africans of the *Antelope* when John Jackson appeared in Savannah with his prisoners on the *Dallas.* He did not contact the Navy to arrange transportation of the Africans directly to Africa. He did not ask whether the law on the sickly months applied to Africans; or if it did not apply to persons in federal custody or slaves, whether it pointed to a hazard which should be considered. He directed Captain Jackson to bring his prize from St. Mary's to Savannah and to deliver the Africans to the care of the United States Marshal for Georgia.

Jackson did as he was told, and the day he set out on his mission of retrieval, a claim was filed on his behalf in the United States District Court for Georgia, suggesting that he was entitled to the federal bounty of $25 per head awarded by the Act in Addition for free Africans, or alternatively was owed salvage on the slaves as Spanish and Portuguese property lost at sea. On July 19, four days after litigation thus began, Habersham reported to Washington on the taking of the *Antelope* and "about 270" Africans. He asked what he should do. In the absence of a Department of Justice or an Attorney General with supervisory responsibilities, he addressed the right hand of the President and focus of executive authority, the Secretary of State.

His letter reached John Quincy Adams in Washington on July 27 and was transmitted on July 28 to the President in Virginia. Adams noted that Habersham's letter "calls for an early answer" and required a decision on "the disposition to be made of the slaves." Adams did not suggest that under the Act in Addition "the slaves" might be free.

Within a week Adams also had reports from Captain Jackson, now back in Savannah, and from John Morel, the United States Marshal, who said he had 258 Africans on hand. These communications, too, he sent on to the President with the comment that if Jackson were to be paid his bounty, it would exhaust the $100,000 appropriation made by Congress for the enforcement of the Act "without taking into account the maintenance in future of the 258 Africans." He did not stop to show how the federal bounty — at $25 per African a maximum of $6,450 — would have exhausted the appropriation. He continued, not resisting the opportunity to make sport of the Act, "and if after all they are to be removed to the Spanish and Portuguese *owners* [his italics or the President's] the affair will exhibit the operation of that law in a light quite unexpected to those who made it. On the other hand, if the 258 Negroes are to be sent to Africa and provided for there at the expense of the United States another appropriation of $100,000 at the next session of Congress will scarcely square the accounts." The suggestion that $200,000 would be the total cost of rescue had a rhetorical ring. While making it, Adams gave Monroe no advice on how the duties laid on the President by the Act to safeguard and support the

Africans could be carried out. He savored the wry twist for the suspended tortoise if the Spanish and Portuguese claim succeeded.

The President's Decision. July — August 1820

Two weeks before the taking of the *Antelope* by a Treasury cutter, Secretary of the Treasury Crawford had addressed the President on the slave trade. As the trade still flourished, Crawford wrote, it was apparent "that our Eastern brethren feel no compunction in buying Negroes to sell again, whatever objections they may have to hold them." Measures had been adopted by Congress, he observed, in relation to this trade. Under the circumstances, he asked, "[w]ould it not be proper to ask Portugal to avoid the "seduction of our citizens from the duty and obedience which they owe to our law?" Nothing in the letter said expressly that "our Eastern brethren" were conducting the slave trade under the flag of Portugal, nothing explicit identified "our Eastern brethren" with Adams' friends in New England, nothing referred to the friendship of the Minister of Portugal with the Secretary of State; but writing to Monroe on a subject so likely to embarrass Adams, Crawford did not need to dot every i.

Two weeks after the arrival of the *Antelope* at St. Mary's, Abbé Correia wrote Adams asking that the President appoint commissioners to meet with the representatives of Portugal to negotiate a settlement of claims for Portuguese shipping taken by privateers of Artigas outfitted in the United States. With this request he submitted a list of sixteen names of Portuguese ships with Portuguese or Brazilian ports of origin, of a total value of $616,158 as ascertained, so he said, in Lisbon "by the proper courts of justice and revised with all care and attention by the Royal Board of Commerce." The general contours of Abbé Correia's request were clear. Particulars were lacking — the owners of the ships, the character of their cargoes, their places of construction, their age and class, their insurers and their insurance, the evidence of their value, as said to be ascertained in Lisbon. Without these particulars the Abbeé's list was scarcely more concrete than his earlier remonstrances.

The relation of this hasty and extraordinary proposal to the taking of the *Antelope* may be but more probably was not coincidental. As a Spanish ship, the *Antelope* was of course not even mentioned. But, as will shortly be seen, the *Antelope* carried property alleged to be Portuguese worth over $40,000 at current prices for slaves. Compensation for such property would legitimately fall within the negotiations Correia proposed if the effect of its capture by the *Columbia* was to deprive its owners of their merchandise. If Correia's tactic succeeded, the owners would be given a route for recovery whatever happened in Savannah and, as Correia stressed generally in writing Adams, a forum independent of the American judiciary. At the very least, the presence of a large new amount of plundered Portuguese property in a state of suspended ownership in Georgia must have been fresh incentive to devise a way of pressing the Executive to aid those who had been plundered.

Adams sent Correia's letter on to Monroe, who with great promptness on July 24 instructed the Secretary of State in the purest presidential style. Adams was told to answer the Abbé "with the best knowledge to be obtained of the facts and most faithful regard to sound principles."

One week later, Abbé Correia traveled to Monticello. It was midsummer, when to go to Virginia was a burden for any traveler. A vital reason must have existed for him, a septuagenarian, to take the trip. Very publicly, he made clear that a vital reason did exist — he had been recalled, he was taking congé of his great Virginia friends, the Presidential Trinity. What more natural obligation, or more pressing? The fact, however, was that he had been recalled almost a year before; in the October following his midsummer expedition, his friends were astonished to discover he was still in Philadelphia; he did not leave the country till November. If he visited Virginia in August to burst, uninvited, upon the President, the necessity of saying adieus could not have been his motive.

The Abbé began his rounds with Thomas Jefferson, to whom, Jefferson reported, he discoursed with eloquence on collaboration between the Portuguese Empire, including in particular Brazil, and the United States, moving Jefferson to declare that he himself would "rejoice to see the fleets of Brazil and the United States riding together as brethren of the same family, and pursuing the same object." When Jefferson as senior statesman had been stirred by this grand vision, the Abbé turned to "the piracies of Baltimore" which had, he said, so gravely wounded Portuguese feelings and interests, and he secured Jefferson's promise to take them up with the President. With Jefferson's sympathies fully enlisted, he moved on to the concrete proposal already broached to Adams and Monroe, his scheme to avoid the American courts by the appointment of presidential commissioners to negotiate Portuguese claims. But he had overreached — the courts could not be so easily circumvented. Jefferson told him "it was out of the question — there could be no such thing." At this response, Abbé Correia became "exceedingly irritable, and talked under high excitement, for which [so Monroe was to be informed] Mr. Jefferson could not account." His inexplicable reaction, it might be inferred, related to his reasons for winning Jefferson to his plan.

Jefferson, however, was only a way to the President himself. Staying at Monticello, the Abbé found it easy to call on Monroe, next door as it were at Albemarle. He did so on August 3, the day of the President's own arrival at Albemarle from Oak Hill, his other Virginia residence. His visit was an extraordinary coincidence. He came on the day the President was making his decision on how he should execute the Act in Addition as it affected the Africans of the *Antelope*.

The President was not unfamiliar with both Savannah and

Captain Jackson of the *Dallas.* In the spring of the previous year he had visited the city and been given a public ball and a public dinner. At the head of the table at the dinner had been an arch of laurels decorated with roses so arranged as to form the letters JAMES MONROE. While toasts were being drunk, the *Dallas* fired salutes. These Maytime scenes may have recurred to him as he drafted his instructions to Adams.

He began, the day of Abbé Correia's visit, as follows:

> I return you Mr. Habersham's letter respecting the capture made by the revenue cutter *Dallas,* Captn Jackson, of a brig under the Artigan flag with about 270 Africans on board. The Dist. Attorneys order to the Captn. to deliver the negroes to the Marshall was I think in strict conformity with the act of 1819. Taking into view the provisions of that act with those of the act of the 15 of May last, page 102, I am inclined to think that all those concerned in the business who were American citizens whether in foreign or American vessels will be considered by the Court as pirates. There will be no security for the safe keeping of these Africans if permitted to go out of the hands of the Marshall nor for the suppression of this nefarious practice without a rigorous execution of the law. The expense of keeping them by the Marshall must be borne. A few strong examples will terminate it with the trade. I think that it will be advisable for you to send Mr. Habersham's letter to the Attorney General & request him to give the District Attorney the necessary instructions for the further prosecution of the business. Instruct the D. Attorney to pursue the affair in its several relations with the utmost attention; — first, to contend for the complete liberation of every African against every claimant, Portuguese, Spaniard or others; and secondly, for the punishment of all concerned in taking them who are exposed to it under our laws. I do not think that any foreigner can sustain a claim against an African brought directly from Africa as a slave, in our Courts, but that when brought within our jurisdiction he must be free. I think that this is in the spirit of our laws, if not more explicitly provided for by them. In any case of doubt it will be proper to take the opinion of the Attorney General who has examined the subject professionally with great care.

The first portion of these instructions up to "for the further prosecution of the business" contained three Presidential wishes couched as suggestions. First, the American citizens involved in the expedition commissioned by José Artigas were to be prosecuted as pirates under the Act of May 15, 1820, a new law, classifying the foreign slave trade as piracy and providing the penalty of death for slave traders. Second, the Africans were not to be let out of the hands of the Marshal. Third, the Attorney General was to direct Habersham in the prosecution. The instructions also contained one Presidential command rebuffing Adams' concern for economy: "The expense of keeping them by the Marshall must be borne."

"Instruct the D. Attorney," the letter continued, "to pursue the affair . . . with the utmost attention." Let the United States "contend for the complete liberation of every African against every claimant, Portuguese, Spaniard, or others." No foreigner could "sustain a claim against an African brought directly from Africa as a slave, in our Courts." The orders were comprehensive and peremptory. The principles asserted were libertarian and humane. The directions which the President gave put the full weight of presidential authority behind the District Attorney, commanding him to fight for the Africans' freedom. The second half of the letter was never sent.

Did Abbé Correia's arrival actually interrupt the writing of the letter? Symbolically such a coincidence would have been appropriate, but it is undeterminable. What is known is that the Abbé came, either during or before the letter's composition, and argued for the appointment of commissioners. On that point Monroe was noncommittal, telling Adams in the same letter, in the Monroe style, to provide "in the most effectual manner in our power for the best interests of our country, and in the mode most consistent with our honor." The President was suspicious — he had heard that the Abbé had even once played South American politics on the revolutionary side; "the very sensitive agent" of Portugal, he had also been "the benefactor" of Spain. In Monroe's judgment, given at the end of August, he was even now "manifestly playing a part from which he expects to gain much credit." Monroe did not speculate in writing as to where the credit would be given or who would give it. He felt the Abbé's "pressure upon us." It was "not generous," considering the way the Abbé had been received. It had a "temper" inconsistent with the Abbé's "profession in other respects." What made him so insistent? Monroe seemed to wonder, and yet concluded, "Be his motive what it may be, the part which we have to act is always the same." So he wrote to Adams a month later, pondering the experience of an August in which the Abbé had kept up his demands on Adams in Washington.

On August 3, at Albemarle, the Abbé so recently a physical presence before him, the ungenerous but not ineffective pressure experienced in his own home, the President reconsidered what he wanted to do in the case involving the claims of Portugal. The first part of the letter was completely pro-Portuguese — a firm stand against the agents of Artigas, who were to be hung as pirates. Only in the second half had he incautiously committed the United States to freeing Spanish and Portuguese slaves. The President crossed out the entire part, beginning with the uncompromising words, "Instruct the D. Attorney." Adams, he now said, should get instructions for the District Attorney from the Attorney General.

The letter, its heart removed, reached Adams on August 7. Three days later Adams asked the Attorney General for his instructions. Only in the case of the prosecution of *The Fourth of July* in Baltimore is William Wirt known to have violated his view of the statutory limits on his duty to advise the President and department heads, not local lawyers of the government. There is no evidence that he treated the President's request in this case as reason to enlarge his scope. He did ask Adams for a copy of the British Parliamentary Papers which contained the pledges of Spain and Portugal to repress the slave trade. Inferably, he investigated whether Spain and Portugal still treated the trade as legal. But he issued no written opinion, and he sent no written instructions to aid the District Attorney.

The same day he wrote Wirt, August 10, Adams also transmitted to Habersham the President's answer, verbatim. He added a single question of his own: Was the John Smith of the *Antelope* the John Smith who had been indicted for piracy in Georgia before? His question, like Monroe's revised letter, focused on the crimes against the Spanish and Portuguese committed by the agents of Artigas. It betrayed not the slightest interest in the disposition of the Africans. In the entire answer to Habersham from Washington, there were no directions on the Africans, except the President's statement that their security depended on their being left with the Marshal.

The District Attorney's Decision. July — August 1820

Alone, without guidance from the President or anyone else in the Administration, Richard Wylly Habersham framed the case for the freedom of the Africans which, for the next seven years, was to occupy the courts of the United States. Litigation had opened on July 15 with the claim filed for Captain Jackson. If the Africans were not free, the property at stake was worth over $75,000 (a prime field hand selling for $700, a newly-arrived slave for half as much), a total sum whose significance may be measured by comparing it with the salary of the Attorney General of the United States (25 times the annual salary) or with what the State of Georgia spent to maintain a Negro in custody (over 1000 times the annual maintenance). Since if the Africans were property they would have to be disposed of by the decree of courts and the aid of lawyers, the fees to be made by counsel in the case were imaginable, and roughly calculable as long as the Africans' treatment as property was assured. Of the thirty white males who composed the bar of Savannah in 1820 and so were eligible to participate in this distribution of potential wealth, approximately one-quarter did. Against them all, their arguments and their self-interest, stood Richard Wylly Habersham.

The best-known of those acting in the case was John Macpherson Berrien. A graduate of Princeton, the grandson of a New

Jersey Supreme Court Justice and a Philadelphia privateer captain, the son of a land claims entrepreneur whom he, when barely nineteen, had defended against charges of swindling the state, he was, like many Georgians of this frontier period, an immigrant to Georgia. He had been a successful private practitioner and State Attorney for the Eastern Circuit and, when the case began, was sole Judge of the Eastern Circuit — in effect, a supreme judge, since the legislature had not established any higher state court. While the case progressed, he became a United States Senator from Georgia and, not long after it was over, Jackson's first Attorney General. He "left an example," the chronicler of the City of Savannah records, "of spotless purity and integrity of life." He was, according to this opinion, "an active member of the legal profession, the virtues of which he illustrated, adorning it by the exhibition of rare and eminent talents." He was, declares Lucius Lamar Knight in his *Reminiscences of Famous Georgians,* justly celebrated as "the American Cicero." By 1820 he had already argued in the Supreme Court of the United States and, though scarcely then a national figure, he towered above most of the bar in power as the judge — he was all his life to be called "Judge Berrien" — and in ability to speak forcefully and act decisively.

Berrien, acting for Captain Jackson on July 15, invoked the jurisdiction of the federal court in admiralty. Beneath the relics of canon law terminology and procedure which admiralty inherited — lawyers were "proctors," claims were "libels," and trial proceeded piecemeal with a liberal use of depositions — a suit in admiralty was a request that the federal judge, William Davies, decide a claim for compensation arising at sea. Asking for salvage on the Spanish and Portuguese slaves and the $25 bounty on the Africans entitled to be free, Berrien did not specify how many fell into each category; but whatever way the case went, the client he had taken could not lose. Salvage would come out of the goods saved, bounty would be paid from the Treasury of the United States. His client and no doubt he too would be better compensated if all the Africans were property.

Harris and Charlton — Charles Harris, the former Mayor of Savannah and present Chairman of the Finance Committee of the city, Thomas Usher Pulaski Charlton, the present Mayor of Savannah — acted for the King of Spain or, more accurately, for Charles Mulvey, Vice Consul in Savannah of the King of Spain. Charlton had had recent experience with an analogous matter and a preview of the case at bar. Two years before, he had advised a state agent rounding up illegally imported Africans that it was "highly probable" that a claim for three of them made in the federal court by a Portuguese resident of the Canary Islands was manufactured for "the convenience of others." He also noted how the practice was weighted in favor of the alleged owner: unless the state was willing to shoulder "the enormous expense" of supporting the slaves, the court would release the slaves to the claimant on "a warrant of appraisement," or bond; so automatic was the practice that the Clerk had already done so, "contemporaneously with the warrant of arrest," to the convenient Canary Islander. This time Charlton's client was a claimant; and, in advance of any judge, he had heard the story of the case by interrogating the *Antelope's* crew in his capacity as Mayor.

The Portuguese claim, put forward in the name of their Vice Consul, Francis Sorrell, was represented by James Morrison and John C. Nicoll, less prominent in Savannah politics than Berrien or Harris or Charlton, but active: Morrison was chairman of two committees (Pump and Market) of the City Council, and was to poll the highest number of votes — 442 — in the aldermanic elections of 1820; Nicoll was elected City Judge of Oyer and Terminer in 1824. Less impressively connected than other counsel, Morrison and Nicoll were still more visible than their nominal client, who was after all not the King of Portugal but the junior partner in the shipping firm of Douglass and Sorrell. In the same way, Harris and Charlton overshadowed the twenty-six-year-old Mulvey. Both vice-consuls were straws, chosen by the lawyers or the claimants of the Africans, and commissioned by Abbé Correia and his Spanish counterpart.

On August 3, the day the President wrote Adams from Albemarle, Harris and Charlton filed their libel, claiming "150 or more" Africans as property of subjects of the King of Spain. In this first effort to tell their story, they said that 100 had been taken from the Spanish at Cabinda, leaving the implication, never later borne out, that another 50 must have been taken from Spanish ships other than the *Antelope*. On the same day, Morrison and Nicoll filed their libel claiming "130 or more" Africans as property of subjects of the King of Portugal. The coincidence of timing, and even more the neat division of what looked like the available supply — 280 — suggested an amicable arrangement between the two kings, or the two vice consuls, or the two law firms, or two undisclosed owners.

In a bar the size of Savannah's, friendly cooperation was essential. Harris, an Englishman who sometimes thought of himself as still an alien, was the "very dear friend" of Berrien, with the friendship running back nine years to the day when Berrien had borrowed his Goldsmith and his Boswell; he was also on excellent terms with Habersham, who later, on leaving for a trip to New York City in 1824, left him as Acting District Attorney in Savannah. Marshal Morel, a coarser character, might not seem to belong to the circle of the bar; nonetheless, in time, he was to be Harris' executor, a position of trust suggesting Harris' regard for him. Harris' partner, Mayor Charlton, had been Berrien's immediate predecessor as State Attorney for the Eastern Circuit, and was soon to succeed him as Judge of the Circuit.

State Judge Berrien had been for six years, from 1804 to 1810, the partner of Federal Judge Davies, and before either was on the bench, they had built up the largest law practice in Savannah, specializing in the representation of creditors from Philadelphia, Boston, and Newport, Rhode Island. Berrien's fourth son, born in 1814, was named for his old partner; and as he was paid only $2100 a year as a state judge, Berrien saw no harm in practicing in the only local court not under his jurisdiction, the federal district court over which Davies presided.

The claimants' opponent, Habersham, was a Savannah native, grandson of the city's first commercial entrepreneur, and the son of a hero of the Revolution. If his status in Savannah was more secure than Berrien's or Harris', he was from the same circle, linked to Berrien in the Union Society, the city's oldest philanthropy, and like him a graduate of Princeton. If he was a member of the Hibernian Society and a St. Patrick's Day orator, Irish ancestry was an asset in Georgia. If he was one of the twenty residents of Savannah in 1820 who contributed to the Colonization Society, this sign of sentiment scarely distinguished him in any radical sense from his colleagues. He was only thirty-four years old. He had been Acting District Attorney for only a year, and Monroe had formally nominated him for the post only in January 1820. The job was half-time, paying $215 per year. His friends at the bar had no reason to expect fierce opposition from him. When he surprised them, it was not by the brilliance of his strategy — he had none — nor by his sense of *noblesse oblige* — they could have anticipated it — but by the tenacity of his resistance.

He had begun, back in July, by responding to Berrien's libel of July 15 with a libel on behalf of the United States, claiming the *Antelope* and her goods as forfeit under the law prohibiting the slave trade. But this action was hasty and done without reading the Act in Addition. He began again on August 15. Faced with the claims of the vice consuls, he did what the President, at Albemarle, had been going to tell him to do but had decided not to tell him. Alone, Richard Wylly Habersham invoked the Act in Addition and asserted that all the Africans — "persons of color" removed from "some one of the Eastern Kingdoms of Africa" by persons intending to sell them in the United States — were free.

The Marshal's Decisions. July — October 1820

The security of the Africans, the President had written, depended on the Marshal — there would be no security for them if permitted to go out of his hands. The Act in Addition designated him as a proper agent to safeguard rescued Africans. The Marshal for the District of Georgia was John Morel, who, of all the persons acting in the legal process to which the Africans were exposed, had probably the greatest physical impact upon their lives. In July, when he became responsible for the refugees of the *Antelope,* he was also advertising the sale of a man, woman and six children whom he would auction on behalf of the Bank of the United States in execution of a judgment. His work had not accustomed him to treat with Africans who were not property. The accommodation he provided for his charges from the *Antelope* was an open space on the race grounds of Savannah, where an impromptu shelter known as "the African encampment" grew up.

How many were there in his custody? According to First Mate Knight of the *Dallas,* he had found 281 when he boarded the *Antelope.* Six died at St. Mary's, three more en route from St. Mary's to Savannah. When the Marshal received them, he reported to Adams that he had "258." Adams noted the difference between Habersham's figure ("about 270") and the Marshal's, and in a letter to Habersham said that he "presumed" that 258 were "all the Africans captured." No one explained the discrepancies between Knight's, Habersham's and the Marshal's figures; and Adams' comment, possibly intended to raise a question, was so mild as to be inaudible to any but the most attentive ear. It did not rouse Habersham to inquiry. Marshal Morel started with responsibility for 258.

On August 3, as the President drafted his instructions and the vice consuls filed their libels, one African disappeared from the camp. Morel presumed that he was stolen and offered a $400 reward for the thief's conviction and the property's return. In his advertisement the Marshal described him, not by name, but by sex — male; by height — 5′6″; and by category — "part of the cargo of the Brig *Ramirez.*"

The President provided for the Africans' maintenance, delegating to the Navy the administration of the appropriation under the Act. From these moneys Morel was to be paid. The Navy began disbursing on August 25, 1820, one month after the Africans had been put in his charge. In the next two years the Navy was to pay the Marshal $20,286.98.

After Habersham filed his assertion that all the Africans were free persons, Mayor Charlton moved that the Africans be released to the claimants on bond in the usual way. Habersham, here following Monroe's instructions, objected. Judge Davies denied the motion. Mayor Charlton then asked the Marshal to put the Africans to work on the fortifications of Savannah. Morel selected 50 "the primest of the gang," and sent them to labor under an overseer for the City of Savannah. A few more were rented out to householders in Savannah. Over 100 were put on the Marshal's own plantation. The Africans were not paid for their labor, but Morel was. It would have been difficult for an observer to have distinguished the lot of the Africans awaiting trial from that of new Negro slaves. In their first six months in Savannah, over one-fifth of them died.

To a degree their deaths were due to their treatment, to a degree to their condition on arrival, and to a degree to the simple fact that they were kept in or near Savannah at a dangerous time. On August 15, the day Habersham claimed the Africans' freedom in court, Mayor Charlton issued a statement to the press denying that any "pestilence" existed in Savannah. One ward was "rather unusually unhealthy," but the disease was "confined principally to strangers and people of intemperate, dissolute habits." The city elections were less than three weeks away; Charlton's popularity was waning; he did not recognize that a catastrophe threatened the city.

On September 2 the Board of Health publicly reported the presence of sixteen dangerous cases of "fever." On September 4 Charlton was re-elected to the City Council, placing fourteenth in an election of fourteen. A week later the Council re-elected him Mayor. Three days later, on September 14 he issued a proclamation: "I feel it my duty to announce to my fellow citizens, and to all whom it may concern, that a mortality prevails in this city, never before experienced, and that the character and type of the fever, is of a malignancy, which renders it prudent for any person, who can make it convenient, to remove beyond the limits of the city's atmosphere." The fever, however, was "not contagious," and "no apprehension ought to be entertained of its being communicated by persons leaving the city." The proclamation became national news when it was reproduced on September 30 by *Niles' Weekly Register.*

A week after announcing the noncontagious fever and the unprecedented mortality, the Mayor put out another statement. The disease had "cast despair around the city and caused its finest population to remove." Still, the Mayor observed, the death toll was largely among nonresidents: 121 of them had died since August; only 26 residents of Savannah had perished.

On October 7 the Mayor publicly advised those who had "very prudently and properly left the city at the beginning of the disease" not to return. On October 10 he publicly referred to "the few remaining inhabitants" and the "disastrous state of things." The catastrophe was now known everywhere. *Niles' Weekly Register* reported on October 21: "*Savannah.* The fever rages with uncommon malignancy in this city — though nearly all of the white population has left it."

The end of the epidemic came in late October. 700 people, white and black, had died. The number of persons, white and black, remaining in Savannah was a little over 1400, out of an original 7000. The Africans of the *Antelope,* to the extent that they had survived, made up a substantial part of the population of the city. The Marshal had his own reasons not to be wasteful of the Africans in his hands, but unless his own plantations were especially salubrious, he had not been particularly vigilant in preventing the newcomers in his care from being ravaged.

The Laughter of James Monroe.
September 1820 — January 1821

Marshal Morel, a presidential appointee, reported directly to John Quincy Adams on a variety of business, chiefly the taking of the census, and his sloppy habit of making the Department of State pay postage due had been punctiliously noted in its records. But Adams had never had occasion to fault his work. "Very judicious and proper" was Adams' appraisal of Morel's accommodations for the Africans when he heard of them. He sent the Marshal's report with this comment — his first words of approbation for anyone connected with the *Antelope* — to the President on September 15.

The Marshal had not mentioned the bulletins of the Board of Health or raised with Adams the question of moving the Africans away from Savannah. But *Niles' Weekly Register* was mandatory reading, in Adams' opinion, for any American diplomat. What happened in Savannah in September and October could not have been a secret in Washington. Neither Adams nor the President was moved to inquire about the health of the Africans whom the United States had "captured" on the *Antelope.*

In November the news reached Washington that Morel himself had been a victim of the plague. The President prepared to appoint a replacement. It was, Adams wrote Morel, "with the highest satisfaction" that the President eventually found the rumor baseless.

Through this period, the Secretary of the Navy, who had been delegated the President's authority under the Act, was Smith Thompson, an American lawyer, the former Chief Justice of the State of New York, and a politician with a strong public position against the slave trade. On January 13, 1821, six months after the Africans' arrival, he wrote Morel to ask him what he had done with them. Their employment had not been mentioned in Morel's September report to Adams. "It is very desirable," Thompson observed, "to save further expenses."

Morel replied that a body of the Africans were employed on public works in Savannah. His reply was transmitted to the President, and clearly raised enough of a problem with Monroe for him to ask for advice from the Attorney General. Wirt's answer, given immediately, read in its entirety as follows:

Office of the Attorney General,
January 27, 1821

Sir: The Act of the 3d March, 1819, in addition to the acts prohibiting the slave trade, places the safe-keeping, support, and removal of the Africans who may thereafter be seized, under the sole and unlimited direction of the President, and appropriates $100,000 to carry the law into effect. If the employment of the Africans in levelling the public works at Savannah was authorized by the President, or now meets his approbation, I can see no objection to his applying to their support, while so engaged, such portion of the sum appropriated as may be necessary for the purpose.

I have the honor to be, etc. etc.

Wm. Wirt

To the President of the United States.

From the letter, it may be guessed what had troubled the President — not the forced labor of persons whom the Government in court said were free, but the maintenance of these laboring Africans at public expense. Wirt quieted Monroe's anxiety. He assumed that the President might approve the forced labor. He assured him that the Africans' safekeeping and support was at his sole and unlimited direction.

On November 12, 1820, John Quincy Adams conferred with the President on the President's Annual Message to Congress. In 1820 the Act in Addition had been given flesh, the United States had assumed responsibility for a substantial body of Africans and had opened litigation in their behalf in the courts of the United States, a number of Africans entrusted to the President's support and safekeeping had died. When he drafted the Message, Monroe knew nothing of his charges' number, health or employment. From the President's perspective, nothing of this sort seemed desirable to know or to bring to the attention of Congress and the nation.

The President mentioned the slave trade once, in the final sentence of the Message, closing a section on the activities of the Navy: "In execution of the law of the last session, for the suppression of the slave trade, some of our public ships have also been employed on the coast of Africa, where several captures have already been made of vessels engaged in that disgraceful traffic." The Act in Addition authorized the President to use the Navy on the coast of Africa, so that it was presumably this law to which the President referred. The *Antelope* had been captured by the Treasury off the coast of Florida, so that it did not appear that the President referred to her capture at all. The Africans at Savannah were passed over in silence.

John Quincy Adams was consulted on Monroe's draft two days before the President sent the Message. He made a solitary comment. He told the President he wished he would add another sentence at the end. He was unwilling, he said, to see the President close his Annual Message with the words "disgraceful traffic." The President did not accept the suggestion but, according to John Quincy Adams, he "laughed heartily at the remark."

· 4 ·

Justice Bridlegoose

Trial One. December 1820

Six months after his capture, John Smith was tried in Savannah for piracy. He had been indicted on three counts: for purloining a hawser worth $20 and a deck awning worth $5 from the unnamed French schooner attacked by the *Columbia*; for the taking of another nameless ship, value $1,000, "alleged to be the property of subjects of the King of Portugal, to the Jurors unknown"; and for taking of the *Antelope*, value $3,000, "alleged to be the property of certain subjects of the King of Spain, to the Jurors unknown."

William Law, State Attorney for the Eastern Circuit and sometime later Judge of the Eastern Circuit, was Smith's counsel. His defense was that Smith was an officer of the Banda Oriental, a government at war. Inconveniently, a certificate from the Collector of Philadelphia had been found in his trunk on the *Antelope* showing that in 1811, aged twenty, he had been certified as an American citizen. Law argued that, since then, Smith had exercised the natural right of expatriation. For four years he had been a countryman of José Artigas.

If this defense were rejected, Smith was still acting, Law maintained, on the basis of a valid commission from a lawful belligerent, and he was no pirate. The Spanish and Portuguese ships were enemy property. The French ship was believed to be carrying munitions to the enemy. Smith had in any event objected to Captain Metcalf that the French vessel should not have been taken, and the *Columbia* had released her after a night.

Drafting the charges, Richard Wylly Habersham had carefully avoided treating the Africans themselves as property taken by theft. Otherwise the indictment showed minimum effort on his part. Smith was not indicted for the capture of the ship which at least one sailor from the *Columbia* had said was the *Exchange* from Bristol, Rhode Island. Failing to charge this act, Habersham missed his best chance of showing an attack on an indisputably American vessel and so made plausible Smith's claim that he only warred on the enemies of Artigas.

Habersham also refrained from trying to show that the apparently Spanish and Portuguese vessels were actually American. In Boston, the owner of the *Science* had recently been prosecuted as an American slaver when the ship's captain was captured with instructions to proceed to San Juan, change the name of the ship to *La Dichosa,* replace the American flag with the Spanish, and take aboard a Spaniard who, the owner said, would be "*capitan de papel*" or nominal captain. Habersham could have read of this successful prosecution in the Savannah *Republican* of November 23, although the details of the fraud were not given. A reader of *Niles' Weekly Register* of December 2 could have read the text itself of the owner's instructions on the "paper" Spanish captain. In the light of *The Science,* it would not have been unreasonable to have explored who Francis Pendergast, the "consignee" seller of the *Antelope,* was. The records of the customs in Savannah itself would have shed at least a little light on the past ownership of the *Antelope.* Without a staff and without any federal agency of investigators, Habersham refrained from being a detective.

Nor did he follow the strong suggestion in the August order of the President that all the Americans captured be indicted for piracy under the Act of May 15, 1820, which equated the foreign slave trade with piracy. Either the District Attorney thought it unfair to charge the commander of the *Antelope* with what became piracy only when he was already embarked upon his criminal enterprise, or it was impossible to get a Georgia grand jury to treat as a capital crime what the Act of May 15, 1820, defined as piracy: the forcible detention of Negroes on the high seas with intent to sell them as slaves. The indictment avoided altogether the criminal significance of the transportation of the Africans.

Habersham's case did not fare well. Davies, the District Judge, did not take seriously the first count, based on the discovery of a French hawser and awning on the *Antelope.* He told the jury that Smith's protest to Metcalf had relieved him of responsibility for this act — even a pirate was permitted a place for repentance which would free him of criminal guilt. As to the second and third counts, the Judge was not disposed to favor the claim that Smith had denaturalized himself, but he was inclined to favor his reliance on the commission from José Artigas. As long as Smith had believed in good faith that he had a commission from "the Artigan government" — even if the commission in fact had not been genuine — then, Judge Davies told the jury, he did not have a piratical intent. The jury acquitted him on all counts.

Released from confinement, Smith entered the civil case in admiralty. On his behalf, Law asked for the return of the *Antelope* and her cargo. All of this property — the Africans were included by implication — was, Law asserted, the prize of a warship of the government of José Artigas. Drafting his libel, he was undeterred by the fact that Artigas himself was now a solitary exile in Paraguay, overthrown by the General Ramirez for whom the *Antelope* had been renamed.

Trial Two. January — February 1821

The trial of the libels of the *Antelope* and the Africans began soon after Smith's acquittal and continued, admiralty fashion, piecemeal, to mid-February. Harris and Charlton produced three witnesses who had been in Savannah since November and had, by court order, toured the town, identifying Negroes from the *Antelope.* They were Raimundo Aribas, Tomás Ximenes and Domingo Grondona. Aribas had been the pilot of the *Antelope* when she sailed from Havana in 1819, Ximenes her boatswain and Grondona, the leader and spokesman in Savannah, her second mate. They and the rest of the crew had gotten passage from Cabinda to San Juan, Puerto Rico, reaching there in June at the same time that their lost ship was heading for the Florida coast. The captain, Grondona said, had died en route. Grondona had carried the story of their misfortunes to the Spanish officials in San Juan and to the owners, Cuesta Manzanal and Brother in Havana. On the abatement of the plague, the trio had been dispatched from Cuba armed with notarized protests against the piracy and notarized documents showing the sale of the *Antelope* by Francis Pendergast, consignee; her registration in the Department of Marine, Cadiz, Spain; and the royal license to acquire new Negroes under which she had acted. Their story formed the substance of the Spanish claim. The Portugese case was far more modest—no documentary evidence, no witnesses of their own, their only argument drawing on the testimony of the *Columbia's* crew that Portugese ships had been attacked and slaves from them acquired.

How many Africans now in Savannah had come originally from the *Exchange,* how many from the *Antelope* at Cabinda? John Smith, claimant of all the Africans, and William Brunton from Smith's ship, put the Portuguese share as "the largest," Smith giving it a specific figure, 210. They made the Spanish share proportionately less, Brunton putting it at 90-odd, Smith at 93. They were contradicted by Grondona and Ximenes, who said there had been 166 slaves on the *Antelope* under her Spanish crew.

On cross-examination by Habersham, Ximenes said he knew the number of Africans aboard because it had been his duty to count them three times a day and to give them one biscuit apiece each morning. Grondona, on cross-examination, said he knew the number because it had been his duty to count them twice a day. He was not asked why he had given no number in his first notarized protest in San Juan and why "166" had become fixed in his mind after he had reached Havana and spoken to Cuesta Manzanal and Brother.

Grondona in his first deposition on December 29 swore that he had recognized 40 of the 166 in his tour of Savannah with the Marshal. In his testimony on February 13 he swore that by then he had recognized 154 of them. No provision had been made in Judge Davies' order for the other parties to the suit to be present when Grondona inspected the Africans, and nothing now was made by Habersham of this striking omission to let him be present at a critical moment. John Smith asked Grondona if he could identify "the small Negroes" from the *Antelope,* and he answered "No." The lawyers did not ask him how he had recognized 154.

Testimony on the number from the *Exchange* was more harmonious. Smith and Brunton both said 25. Brunton added that all were men or boys. His testimony was the only allusion to gender among the Africans. Smith said that 16 or 18 of these had died or drowned before the *Dallas* had made her capture, Brunton said 10 or 12. These were the only statements assigning specific losses to a specific group of Africans, those from the sole slaver identified as American, and they were not controverted.

The United States was "a mere nominal claimant," Richard Wylly Habersham told the court. "The negroes are the actual party." He made no request that an interpreter be found so that the Africans themselves might testify. The Africans did not appear in person before the court. Their case rested on the legal conclusions Habersham drew from the testimony of Jackson and Knight that they had intercepted the *Antelope* heading for an American port carrying enchained Negroes, and from the abundant testimony of the *Columbia's* crew that it had been recruited in Baltimore.

In oral argument Habersham systematically attacked the basis on which each claimant sought the Africans as property. Smith, he said, could not maintain his claim because of his illegal outfitting in Baltimore, as the proctors of Spain and Portugal also argued. Smith was, moreover, an American citizen found on the high seas with Africans in his possession. Habersham had not secured a criminal indictment on these grounds, but he thought it proper to urge them in the civil case: "from the moment he took these negroes into his possession and proceeded in search of a market for them," Habersham argued, "he became engaged in the slave trade."

Secondly, Habersham declared, the Spanish and Portuguese claims had to meet a high standard of proof. *Prima facie,* British admiralty precedents — *The Amédie, The Fortuna* — showed that the slave trade was regarded as illegal everywhere. Slave traders must prove that it was legal where they engaged in it. This the Spanish had failed to do. Under the treaty signed with England on September 23, 1817, Spain had agreed that any slaver operating south of the equator must have a special license from the King. The license had not been produced. Its absence raised the presumption that the Spanish flag "was used to cover the property of citizens of other countries who cannot lawfully engage in the trade." The Portuguese had also failed to meet the requisite standard of proof: "there is no evidence whatever of Portuguese ownership — the actual claimants are unknown — the names of the vessels unknown — no papers, no documentary evidence, none of the original crew of the Portuguese vessels to give evidence. The claimant has had six months to produce evidence of Portuguese ownership. The absence of all evidence, where evidence might have been procured, is itself a circumstance of strong suspicion." Short on witnesses of his own, Habersham put the case for the Africans as well as reasoned argument could. If he forgot to make the Spanish and Portuguese identify their property, he struck at a central weakness of the Portuguese case when he pointed out that no Portuguese owner had been identified.

Opinion and Judgment. February — March 1821

William Davies, United States District Judge for the District of Georgia, was a past president of the Union Society and regarded as an exemplary member of the Protestant Episcopal Church. No college or law school man, he had begun his working life as a commercial clerk and then served an apprenticeship in law in the chambers of a local judge and been elected to the legislature from Liberty County. When his prosperous partnership with Berrien had ended through Berrien's becoming a judge, he had practiced by himself, becoming in 1817 the United States District Attorney. His patron was Secretary of the Treasury Crawford, who thought him a man of excellent character, and in due course President Monroe awarded him the federal judgeship, a post not locally regarded as exacting: "impaired health," so his obituary was to recall, "disposed him to retire from private practice and accept appointment to the federal bench." He was only forty-four, and the salary was $1500.

He gave his decision on February 21, 1821, five days after the testimony was completed. The day before the decision was announted it became known that Judge Berrien had resigned his state judgeship. That this resignation should be linked to the case and to Judge Davies also resigning, leaving a post he had only held two years, was not known.

Judge Davies began by disposing of the claim of John Smith, following one part of Habersham's argument without touching on Smith and the slave trade. Almost all of Smith's crew, he held, had been shown to be Americans taken on in Baltimore. Recruitment was clearly a breach of American neutrality. As Supreme Court Justice Bushrod Washington had decided in 1805 in *The Alerta,* captures by a ship which was in violation of American neutrality would not be recognized in an American court. John Smith should take nothing.

To Habersham's main argument against the Spanish and Portuguese, Judge Davies responded with a disquisition on the legality of the slave trade. "However inhuman" the slave trade was, Judge Davies observed, it was not illegal under international law. "However obnoxious it is to every benevolent feeling," Judge Davies said, the slave trade was legal except in countries where it was specifically forbidden. "Notwithstanding its injustice," Judge Davies wrote, unless a government had banned it, the slave trade gave rise to property rights.

Spain, he went on, had not been shown to ban the trade south of the equator by a specific royal decree. An American court would not enforce the Spanish treaty with England for the benefit of Africans not privy to the agreement. The license to trade for new Negroes issued in Cuba to Cuesta Manzanal and Brother, and submitted as documentary evidence by counsel, was in any event sufficient proof of compliance with the conditions of the treaty. As for the Portuguese claimants, "the circumstances in which the property was found" were enough. The sailors from the *Columbia* had testified that a portion of the Africans had been in the possession of Portuguese ships off the coast of Africa. Possession at such a place proved ownership.

The Judge went on to consider the possibility, not sharply raised by Habersham, that the Spanish and Portuguese owners had been affected by John Smith's illegal taking of their property and his subsequent run to the United States. On this point Davies considered he had apt teaching from the Supreme Court in the case of *The Josefa Segunda,* decided only the year before. The Court had held that a capture of Spanish slaves by a revolutionary privateer transferred the ownership to the privateer. When the privateer was caught trying to smuggle the slaves into New Orleans, the slaves were forfeit. It would have been different, the Supreme Court had said, if the captor of the Spanish slaves had been a mere pirate, since it would have been "unreasonable and unjust to visit upon the innocent owners of the property the sins of a pirate." By analogy, Judge Davies thought, capture by a revolutionary privateer which had breached the neutrality law should be treated like capture by a pirate. It would be unreasonable and unjust to visit the sins of John Smith upon innocent slave traders from Portugal and Spain.

Judge Davies came to the part of his opinion the litigants were waiting for, the disposition of the property. The Vice Consul of Portugal should take the Africans from the Portuguese ships; the Vice Consul of Spain should take the *Antelope* and the Africans who had first been on the *Antelope;* Captain Jackson should be paid salvage on this property which he had retrieved. One batch remained to be disposed of — the Africans taken from the *Exchange* of Bristol, Rhode Island. They were allotted to the United States. Captain Jackson and his crew were decreed the legal bounty of $25 per head on them.

One question was not decided by Judge Davies: How many fell to each share? He ordered the Clerk to report the total number in the Marshal's possession, to distinguish the Portuguese and Spanish Africans in this number, and to determine the amount owed as salvage.

On Washington's Birthday, 1821, Marshal Morel reported the number of Africans on hand. He had received 258 on July 24, 1820; he now had 212. One had disappeared, the small male for whom the reward had been posted; one had been "judicially discharged," a curious and unexplained description when the African was seeking his freedom; and 44 had died — the Marshal did not say when, or how. George Glen, the Clerk, did not inquire further. He took it as given that he had 212 to divide.

His calculations and their sources were as follows:

Africans on the *Antelope* at Cabinda	-	93	(John Smith)
Africans on the *Exchange*	-	25	(Smith, Brunton)
Africans from Portugese ships	-	213	(Smith's figure increased by 3)
Africans originally taken		331	

"Average loss" of Spanish slaves - 32%	=	30	
Net Spanish salves	=	63	
"Average loss" of Portugese slaves - 33%	=	71	
Net Portugese slaves	=	142	
"Average loss" of American slaves - 71%	=	18	(American average loss reached by deducting from 25 the 16 specific deaths mentioned by Smith and then subtracting 2 more)
Net American slaves	=	7	

Value as appraised by Clerk Glen and Oliver Hayes and H.W. Hills, merchants:

Spanish slaves (63 × $300 per head)	=	$18,900
Portugese slaves (142 × $300 per head)	=	$42,600
Less: Salvage to Captain Jackson (25% of property)	=	$15,225
Bounty owed Captain Jackson by Treasury (7 free Africans × $25)	=	$175

On March 6, Judge Davies confirmed the Clerk's allocations, appraisals and report. Three days later he submitted his resignation to the President. A week later, Judge Davies and Judge Berrien prepared an announcement for the press. They had, they said, "reunited their professional interests in the practice of law and have taken an office in Shad's building." As Judge Davies' obituary put it, "The claims of a numerous family" had "again called him to the bar." The President accepted his resignation on May 2, 1820, a little less than two months after the partnership had been formed. In the subsequent affairs of the partnership, Davies appeared as a subordinate partner. He named his youngest child, born sometime after these events, Macpherson Berrien Davies.

Appeal. March — May 1821

Six days after Judge Davies' decree had confirmed the Clerk's Report, Richard Wylly Habersham wrote John Quincy Adams as follows:

> The number remaining in the hands of the Marshal of those brought in is now reduced by death to two hundred and twelve. The expense already incurred for the maintenance of these negroes is so great and that which will be incurred if they remain longer will be so onerous to the government that although myself not well satisfied with the opinion and decree of the District Judge, particularly of so much thereof as decrees the great proportion of the negroes to the Portuguese Vice Consul, I have hesitated to appeal from that decree. Upon mature consideration I have now however determined to appeal and have consequently done so, in behalf of the government. In order however that the government may judge for itself whether under the circumstances of the case there is such probability of ultimate success in favor of the liberty of these people as to authorize the incurring of so great an expense for their support, I have deemed it proper to submit such papers as may be necessary for the formation of a correct opinion.

He had hesitated; he had calculated at least the financial costs; and he had taken the initiative.

Adams received, with this letter, a copy of Judge Davies' opinion and a copy of Habersham's argument to the court. He commented on neither, nor did he, so far as appears, transmit them, or Habersham's letter, to the President. He made no connection between the decision and Judge Davies' resignation, dispatched to Adams almost simultaneously with Habersham's report. Neither he nor the President gave any answer to Habersham. If "the government" judged for itself that the appeal was worth pursuing, silence was its mode of signaling its approval.

The appeal was argued on Tuesday, May 8, 1821 before the Sixth Circuit Court sitting in Milledgeville, the state capital of Georgia. Habersham continued to act for the United States, and Judge Berrien, now of Berrien and Davies, for Captain Jackson. In theory the Portuguese and Spanish had conflicting interests, but the actual collaboration between them was underlined by Mayor Charlton appearing for both Vice Consuls to attack the size of the salvage awarded. William Law gave up on John Smith's case, no one appeared for him, and his appeal was dismissed without consideration.

The Sixth Circuit Court consisted of one Justice of the Supreme Court, riding circuit, and the District Judge. As the District Judge's resignation had been accepted too recently to fill the vacancy, the Justice of the Supreme Court sat alone. He was William Johnson, a native of Charleston, South Carolina, a graduate of Princeton, a law clerk in Charleston, South Carolina, a state legislator when he was twenty-two, a judge of the highest court of the state when he was twenty-seven, an appointee of Thomas Jefferson to the Supreme Court when he was thirty-three, and a justice of the Supreme Court for the past seventeen years. A "large, athletic well-built man" of fifty "with a full, ruddy and fair countenance," Justice Johnson had the assurance of one who has been a judge since he was a young man and will be a judge for the rest of his life, an independence of temper which ran to idiosyncracy, and strong feelings which he habitually expressed in solemn moral terms. From him almost any result might have been expected. He gave his decision on Friday of the week of the argument.

"Case of the *Antelope* otherwise the *Ramirez* and cargo," Justice Johnson entitled his opinion. The suit had been brought, he said, by John Jackson "on behalf of the United States and officers and crew of the cutter *Dallas* who claim the vessel and cargo as forfeited under the act of the 20th April, 1808, or under the modern law of nations on the subject of the slave trade" — a remarkable description of the action, ignoring the crucial role of the Act in Addition and burying the claim for the freedom of the Africans in the claim put forward by Jackson.

At the heart of the case, Justice Johnson thought, was the status of the slave trade in international law. English judges, he observed, were inclined to treat the slave trade as illegal by the law of nations. But the precedents were recent and tainted. They went back only to the successful slave revolt in San Domingo and the British perception that new slaves could swell the slave population of the British West Indies to the danger point. From this time, "philanthropy like the pent up vapor began freely to diffuse itself and extend its spread over the British courts of vice-admiralty." After England had prohibited the trade by act of Parliament, she had a commercial reason for wanting every country to stop it: Jamaica must compete with Cuba. The desires of England, rooted in fear and avarice, did not create a new law of nations.

No narrow interest, Justice Johnson suggested, determined his own view of international law. He had studied moral philosophy at Princeton with Witherspoon, he was a Jeffersonian: "That slavery is a national evil, no one will deny except him who would maintain that national wealth is the supreme good." A materialist of the latter sort was beneath the contempt of a moralist in the style of Thomas Jefferson. Beyond merely material considerations, it would be his task to discover the law.

Like Judge Davies, Justice Johnson employed the dependent clause to pay tribute to the principle his main predicate was about to deny: "However revolting to humanity may be the reflection," he wrote, "the laws of any country on the slave trade are nothing more in the eyes of any nation than a class of the trade laws of the nation that makes them." Under international law the slave trade was legal. A judge of the United States could not enforce the commercial code of the United States against subjects of Spain and Portugal peacefully trading in foreign waters. Slave traders could recover their property, unlawfully taken from them, in the courts of the United States, and so should these. The Vice Consul of Spain should have his property at once if he would put up a bond to remove the Negroes from the country and to pay his share of the salvage.

The Vice Consul of Portugal, Justice Johnson held, had not proved his case: no Portuguese owners had been identified. He did not, however, dismiss the Portuguese case for want of evidence or want of a proper party. Two months earlier in the Supreme Court itself, in the case of *The Bello Corrunnes,* he had given the Court's opinion, rejecting the contention of the Attorney General that a Spanish Vice Consul could not sue to recover property taken by a revolutionary privateer. A "vice-consul, duly recognized by our government," he had written, "is a competent party to assert or defend the rights of property of the individuals of his nation, in any court having jurisdiction of causes affected by the application of international law. To watch over the rights and interests of their subjects, wherever the pursuits of commerce may draw them, or the vicissitudes of human affairs may force them, is the great object for which consuls are deputed by their sovereigns; and in a country where laws govern, and justice is sought for in courts only, it would be a mockery, to preclude them from the only avenue through which their course lies to the end of their mission." The Vice Consul of Portugal in Savannah, Justice Johnson now thought, was not to be mocked. He was to be given an opportunity to produce more proof at the next session of the court, to be held in Savannah, seven months later.

On salvage, Justice Johnson split the difference between the $75 in Davies' decree and the $25 Mayor Charlton had argued should be the limit. At $50 apiece, Jackson would still receive $9000 if the Portuguese sustained their claim, although the maximum Portuguese share had been reduced by correcting the Clerk's application of average loss to the American share. The average loss, Johnson held, should have been applied to the original number taken off of the *Exchange.* Setting that loss at 34%, he subtracted 9 from 25 and ruled 16 to be the portion of the United States.

93 Africans for the Spanish, up to 132 for the Portuguese, 16

free, up to $10,200 salvage and bounty to Jackson — such was Justice Johnson's result. But who was free and who was property? Asking this question, skipped by Judge Davies and the Clerk, Johnson expressed puzzlement. "I can," he wrote, "decree freedom to a certain number, but I may decree that to A which is the legal right of B. It is impossible to identify the individuals who were taken from the American vessel, and yet it is not less certain that the benefit of this decree is their right and theirs alone. Poor would be the consolation to them to know that because we could not identify them we have given away their freedom to others."

In this dilemma Justice Johnson turned to the method recommended in Rabelais by Justice Bridlegoose whose "marvelously long-continued happy Success in the Judiciary Results of his Definitive Sentences," Pantagruel explains, is caused by "the favorable Aspect of the Heavens, and Benignity of the Intelligences; who out of their love to Goodness, after having contemplated the pure Simplicity and sincere Unfeignedness of Justice Bridlegoose in the acknowledgment of his Inabilities, did regulate that for him by Chance, which by the profoundest Act of his maturest Deliveration he was not able to reach unto." So aided, Justice Bridlegoose maintained that "Chance and Fortune are good, honest, profitable and necessary for ending of and putting a final Closure to Dissentions and Debates in Suits at Law." Justice Johnson proceeded in a spirit which made Chance and Fortune the instruments of God. "We can only do the best in our power," he wrote, "the lot must direct their fate; and the Almighty will direct the hand that acts in the selection."

Execution. July 1821

At Savannah on July 18, 1821, 204 men, women, and children, the present survivors of the *Antelope* — 8 had died or disappeared in the past six months — were assembled. Richard Wylly Habersham appointed his relation Joseph Habersham, an apothecary, to act for the United States. The Spanish and Portuguese Vice Consuls did not appear. Marshal Morel was in attendance. Joseph Habersham drew 16 winning numbers.

For the first time in the judicial record of the case it was necessary to name some of the Africans as human beings. They were all males, since, as only men and boys had come from the *Exchange*, Justice Johnson had directed that only males could be winners. The Clerk recorded their names: Mingo, number 102, was first; Major, number 2, was the sixteenth. Sam, Horace, January, Tawney, Ned, Paul, John, Bill, another Mingo, Dick, Chance, another John, Boatswain and Tony were also certified to the Clerk of the Court as winners of the lottery and so entitled to liberty.

An official account of the proceedings was sent to Adams by Habersham along with Justice Johnson's decree. Writing four days after he had participated in the game, Habersham wrote, "I have deemed it not advisable to appeal on behalf of the United States." Silence again followed from Washington.

Compensation. December 1821 — January 1822

In the Christmas season, 1821, the Sixth Circuit Court met at Savannah to decree the disposition of "the residue of the Africans." Justice Johnson was now joined by the new District Judge, Jeremiah Touche Cuyler. The descendant of a New York family of Dutch Huguenots who had moved to Savannah, fifty-three years old and the father of eleven children, Judge Cuyler was the successor to Mayor Charlton as the Grand Master of the Georgia Masons.

Charlton himself had succeeded Judge Berrien by again becoming Judge of the Eastern Circuit, the post he had vacated to enter Savannah politics. Alderman Morrison resumed the task of representing the Vice Consul of Portugal, with the burden of producing evidence of Portuguese ownership. He produced none. If Johnson's opinion of May was followed, the Portuguese were now out of court. Johnson and Cuyler in December were not so severe: the Portuguese share was merely reduced and the Spanish share increased at its expense. Johnson and Cuyler now accepted Grondona and Ximenes' figure of 166 as the number they counted daily on the *Antelope.* On this basis the remaining Africans were to be divided between the Vice Consul of Spain and the Vice Consul of Portugal in the proportions 166/296 and 130/296. They were to be divided into a human dividend of 188 — a dividend 16 less than in July.

It was natural at this point in the proceedings, after a year of litigation, for counsel to think of interim compensation. Habersham had agreed that he would not appeal the part of the decree disposing of the *Antelope* herself to the Vice Consul of Spain. She was accordingly sold for $750 — no doubt she had been battered by her last voyage — and the proceeds were divided $300 to Charlton, $300 to Harris, and $150 to Judge Berrien, who, up to this point where compensation was awarded, had not appeared as counsel for the Vice Consul of Spain.

Habersham had decided not to appeal the lottery and agreed not to appeal the disposition of the ship. But the disposition of the Portuguese claim still troubled him. Now, after the judge's final decree, he again addressed Adams and the silence of the Administration. He wrote on January 8:

> Notwithstanding however that in these cases decrees have gone against the United States both in the District and Circuit Courts I have ventured on behalf of the United States to enter an appeal to the Supreme Court and have endeavored by every means in my power to prepare a case for the final hearing at the approaching Term of that Court. The expenses are very heavy and are daily increasing. Conscientiously believing however that these people are entitled to their freedom I have not waited for instructions from the government respecting the propriety of an appeal but trust that my conduct will meet with the approbation of the President. I have this day written to the Attorney General and have furnished him with a statement of the case.

Without material assistance from the Administration, without encouragement from the President or the Secretary of State or the Attorney General, in the face of the resort to chance decreed by a Justice of the Supreme Court, Richard Wylly Habersham sought to bring the case of the Africans before the highest court in the land.

· 5 ·

"If He Was A Man That Could Turn A State Or Perhaps Even A County . . ."

La Jeune Eugénie. September — December 1821

In the fall of 1821 a second "Antelope" appeared in Boston, without the human interest and legal complications of recaptured Africans but with the potentiality of decisively affecting the treatment of the slave trade by the Supreme Court. *La Jeune Eugénie* was a slaver captured, empty, off the coast of Africa by an American naval vessel, the *Alligator,* Lieutenant Robert Stockton, commander. He brought her into Boston for condemnation. She was established to be American-built, but her name and her flag were French and she had been registered in Guadaloupe, the French colony from which, perhaps coincidentally, the Bristol slavetrading family of DeWolfe had sprung. A French Vice Consul in Boston duly appeared on her behalf, objecting to an American judge even taking jurisdiction to decide the ownership of a French vessel. The District Attorney informed Adams that he was confident that Joseph Story, the Supreme Court Justice sitting as the Circuit Judge in Boston, would condemn the ship as American.

Stockton's father, a New Englander, came to take a cynical view of what would happen: his son "ought to know that as long as the Central Govt is under absolute Southern influence there can be no bona fide wish to put an end to the Slave Trade." But it was Adams who was clearest on how Stockton should be repudiated. When he first heard of the case in September, 1821, Adams had been incensed at Stockton's conduct. His first thought had been that Stockton should lose his command and the Secretary of the Navy should peremptorily issue general orders "against capturing vessels under any flag than that of the United States." On second thought, as Stockton as a person entered his range of vision, he did not favor punishing him personally for his zeal; but he insisted that the Navy be restrained. The President agreed as to the naval orders and, eventually, peremptory orders were issued to the Navy not to intercept vessels "under any other than the American flag." Monroe also came to the conclusion that *La Jeune Eugénie* should be surrendered to France, eliciting a mild protest from his Attorney General. "You have certainly taken the safe side," Wirt advised him, "as it affects our questions of search with Great Britain. But *quaere* whether you are not too far within the line. That vessels are in the constant habit of using the flags of all nations to cover their illicit operation is familiarly and universally understood . . ."

As the President pondered this advice, Adams wrote from Quincy, "I am satisfied of the expediency of the delivery over of the *Jeune Eugénie* to the French Consul." He did not want to be unfair to Stockton who would thereby lose his prize; but neither did he see any difficulty in getting a federal court to comply with the President's wishes.

After the argument in Boston and before Story had given his decision, the Cabinet met on November 3 to discuss the case. Adams proposed that the District Attorney be instructed to tell the court that the President, after hearing the position of the Minister of France, considered the vessel subject only to the jurisdiction of a French tribunal. Secretary of the Navy Thompson opposed Adams' suggestion, and the Attorney General questioned its wisdom. Three days after the Cabinet meeting, Wirt took up the matter again, telling Adams plainly that if "the mere hoisting of a foreign flag or show of foreign papers precluded all inquiry," then "the Act of Congress was of no avail," and all legislation against the slave trade was "vanity." It was "notorious that the slave trade was now carried on by many of our citizens under cover of Spanish and French names and papers." Adams replied that the question was "whether in time of peace the commander of a public vessel of one nation has a right to *board* [his italics] the merchant vessels of another." Congress could not authorize an American warship to board a foreign ship. "By the law of nature," Adams wrote in his Diary, "no vessel has a right to board another at sea without its consent." The law of nature as to maritime rights evidently overruled any law of Congress on the suppression of the slave trade.

At a second Cabinet meeting on *La Jeune Eugénie,* on November 8, 1821, the Secretary of State continued to maintain that "the flag must be considered as the protection of the vessel from being even boarded in time of peace." Thompson and Wirt still did not agree, but Wirt was willing to compromise. He furnished the President with a written opinion that if he, the President, was satisfied that Stockton's seizure of the ship had been a violation of French sovereignty, the President could lawfully return the ship to France. In other words, if the President were willing to treat the flag a vessel flew as decisive of her nationality, he could put into effect the policy the President and Adams had favored from the start. Armed with this opinion, Adams did not delay. The District Attorney was instructed to convey to Justice Story that the President desired that *La Jeune Eugénie* be surrendered to France.

In Boston, Story was in the process of drafting his opinion, knowing that there was a distinct possibility of presidential intervention. He had been informed that the case had been the subject of diplomatic exchanges between the United States and France. He considered what his response should be to the President. An American judge could neither be blindly obedient to the desire to extinguish the slave trade nor blindly obedient "to the wishes of any sovereign." A court — Story transposed the individual judge into the impersonal institution — must "decide fearlessly and let its errors, if any, be corrected by a higher tribunal." A "court of justice in this country has its path clearly marked out and defined. However delicate or painful its predicament it cannot seek shelter under the wings of executive authority . . ." With this preamble, Story seemed to proclaim a determination to decide the case and not to turn over the ship to France.

Story went on to dismiss the President's and Secretary of State's view that every national flag was sacrosanct. His view was what Wirt had already put to the President: Unless you could investigate "foreigners engaged in the fraudulent cover of your own subjects," he observed, the ocean "would be a sanctuary for all sorts of offenses." In the case of the slave trade, if American citizens were involved, "they would conceal their interests under a foreign flag and passports, and wear disguises which might facilitate their designs and favor their escape from punishment." It was right for officers of the United States to penetrate the disguises. It was right for a court to demand more proof of foreign ownership than a flag, foreign papers and alleged owners. Concretely, if the French were to establish themselves as owners of a ship not long ago registered as American, they should produce a bill of sale, show what they had paid and disclose the names of the American sellers.

But even if the French met these tests, Story went on, they could not recover in his court. Since the fall of 1819, he had been lecturing federal grand juries in New England — in Portland, not far from where the *Antelope* had been built; in Boston, where New England capital accumulated; in Providence, near the very seat of the slave trade — on what the trade was like.

Relying on the reports of British anti-slavery advocates, Story had a very clear secondhand conception of the business. Kidnapped from their villages, Africans were stowed on the slavers "like lumber." In his view the simile was exact, not hyperbolic. In the best-regulated ships a grown man was allowed but 16 inches in width, 32 inches in height, and 5 feet, 11 inches in length. The slaves were fettered and wedged close together, so that "the utmost disorder arises from endeavors to relieve themselves in the necessities of nature; and the disorder is still further increased by the healthy being not infrequently chained to the diseased, the dying, and the dead." This human suffering was not the work of natural disasters, but inflicted by "man on man." "How could we," Story had asked the New Englanders, apologize for "an indifference to this subject?" Americans were "steeped to their mouths in this stream of iniquity." New Englanders thronged to the coasts of Africa "under the stained flags of Spain and Portugal." They brought their human cargoes to the Southern ports of the United States, "there under the forms of law, defeating the purpose of the law itself, and legalizing their inhuman, but profitable adventures." Story called on New England's belief in a Christian God and inquired "May not the miserable African ask, 'Am I not a man and a brother?'"

With these perceptions of the evil to be eradicated, Story turned to the French claim on the supposition that *La Jeune Eugénie* was actually French. She had been engaged in an "incurably unjust and inhuman" practice, a trade "that carries away at least 50,000 persons annually from their homes and their families," a traffic that began "in corruption and plunder and kidnapping" and created wars; that exploited the innocent and the defenseless; that stood, therefore, "reprehended by the present sense of nations." With this conclusion, Story converted ugly facts and moral outrage into a legal holding. If the present sense of nations reprehended the slave trade, it was illegal everywhere — illegal not by the laws of the United States or of France (though France, too, outlawed the business), but by international law, the law of nations. The French owners who claimed through the Vice Consul were guilty of legal wrong under whatever flag they had acted. They could not enter an American court and ask that justice be put to work to recover the engine of their crime. Between the time this opinion was so bravely begun and the time it was finished, Story changed his mind. He left untouched the strong preamble, the refusal to hide behind the wings of the Executive; he left untouched — to be greeted with praise by the American Colonization Society — his analysis of the slave trade; he left standing — to be used later against Justice Johnson's opinion in *The Antelope* — the conclusion that the slave trade was internationally unlawful. But he changed the end, or what must have been the end if he had completed what he had begun. Before his draft was done, the District Attorney at Monroe's direction had given up the case. Story announced that he would accede to the suggestion of the President, made "at a late period in this cause" — what bitterness that "late period" contained! — and turn over *La Jeune Eugénie* to the Vice Consul of France, surrendering the court's jurisdiction. A French appeal to the Supreme Court, which would have reached the Court in the same term *The Antelope* came from Georgia, was forestalled. The Monroe Administration stood committed to the sanctity of the flag the ship flew.

Postponement. February—March 1822

The Antelope was docketed in the Supreme Court on February 21, less than two months after Habersham had filed his appeal. The record of what had happened below — the opinions of Judge Davies and Justice Johnson, the Clerk's reports, the judges' orders, the documentary evidence, parts of the testimony — were transcribed and filed with the Court. The case was ripe, as the agricultural metaphor of the law has it, for argument and decision. Half of the Court's six-week term, in which argument was annually heard, remained. If the case was not argued in February or March 1822, it must be put over to February or March 1823. In that term, the Supreme Court retreated from an earlier softness toward South American revolutionary activity, and the representatives of Spain and Portugal were generally victorious. The *Gran Para,* the *Monte Allegre* and the *Raniha de los Anjos,* prizes of privateers commissioned by José Artigas in the name of the Banda Oriental, were held to have been taken illegally and were awarded to various vice consuls of Portugal. The *Santissima Trinidad* and the *St. André* were denied to privateers commissioned by the United Provinces of the Rió de la Plata and given to a vice consul of Spain. The *Arrogante Barcelones* was held to be the illegal prize of a ship commissioned by Buenos Aires, and awarded to another vice consul of Spain. *The Antelope,* however, was not judged at all.

When one has observed the President and his Secretary of State, against opposition from within the Cabinet itself, override the objections of the Attorney General and compel a strong-minded Justice of the Supreme Court, armed with moral fervor, to do their will to establish the principle that foreign flags may not be challenged by ships of the United States, is it necessary to ask why *The Antelope* was not judged? Habersham had, against what he himself had indicated in July, taken the appeal. The Administration would not disavow it utterly; after all, the presence of the Africans and the operation of the Act of Addition made the case more complex than that of *La Jeune Eugénie.* But having fought so successfully to keep a court from encroaching on foreign policy, the Administration had no desire to have its Attorney General argue to the Supreme Court, especially when that Court was busy restoring Spanish and Portuguese shipping, that the flags of Spain and Portugal which had waved above the heads of the Africans from the *Antelope* were not decisive criteria of ownership.

To the considerations of foreign policy were added domestic political ones as the Administration emerged from the great crisis over the admission of Missouri. Monroe had acquiesced in the Act in Addition and the Colonization Society's interpretation in 1819. In 1820 he had been able to visualize the country splitting, the western states aligned with the northeastern states and the line of division drawn at the Potomac. Even as Congress was presently constituted, he observed, power was held by the free states "if many members from those states did not vote against the sense of their constituents." From the perspective of a southern politician interested in preserving the Union and perpetuating southern control of the government, any cause which focused feelings on the rights of slaves could be seen as inflammatory. That the Act in Addition might arouse the slaves had been remarked by Wirt when he was first asked to interpret it by Key. Now that a case under the Act had come to Washington, the President must have seen what events in Georgia in 1825 were to confirm — this sort of issue, argued in a national forum, had an even greater potential for inflaming politicians.

The sensitivity of the President, whose security, to be sure, was Olympian, had to be less than that of any man whose chance of becoming President depended on transcending a region. If Monroe did not want to divide the country, still less did Adams. "In respect to candidates for the President," Joseph Story wrote in February, "discussion has somewhat abated, but it is clear that all public business is coloured with hues borrowed from this subject. — The Cabinet is by the ears. All are candidates . . ." Story wrote as an observer, but from one who had so recently experienced the power of the President, the comment on the coloring of "all public business" had a special bite. Story, it appears, had reflected on Adams' part in the decision not to let *La Jeune Eugénie* move through the American courts.

The Administration also saw — Attorney General Wirt pointed it out — that the upshot of *La Jeune Eugénie* made it possible to avoid more "*Antelopes*" popping up to embarrass the conduct of foreign policy and disturb domestic harmony. A case immediately rose to demonstrate the desirability of preventing this sort of litigation. *La Pensée* was brought by the warship *Hor-*

net into New Orleans in January 1822, with 220 Africans aboard — the first large batch to be rescued since the *Dallas* had taken the *Antelope.* The Minister of France, Hyde de Neuville, informed Adams that *La Pensée* was a French ship, in the hands of pirates when taken by the *Hornet.* It looked as though all the issues in *The Antelope* would be litigated again — except that, as the French Minister said that the Africans would be returned "to their native land," human liberty did not appear at issue. Wirt advised the President that he had the authority to hand over "the vessel with her cargo" without waiting for a court order. That authority had been "determined" by Justice Story's decision in *La Jeune Eugénie.* Wirt no longer stood by the advice he had tendered the President before *La Jeune Eugénie* was decided.

The "only difficulty in the case," Wirt found, came from supposing that the Africans must be treated like free Europeans. But that supposition was false: "the introduction of Africans into our country is expressly forbidden by law." The President could dispose of them by executive authority to the diplomat who asked for them. Nothing in Wirt's opinion indicated that he was restrained by the directives of the Act in Addition. The Act in Addition pointed to the total exclusion of Africans. Wirt could not have looked forward to arguing *The Antelope.* What could be gained by winning it if the main purpose of the Act in Addition was to keep Africans out of the country?

Wirt had an apoplectic stroke which kept him from arguing any cases in the February Term, 1822; but co-counsel — even Habersham — could have been authorized to take his place. *The Antelope* was not argued in the 1822 term because the Administration did not want it argued.

Morel Accused. December 1821 — October 1822

Afternoon, December 18, 1821: the President and John Quincy Adams discussed the United States Marshal in Savannah. John Morel, Marshal of the District of Georgia — John Morel, M.D.G., as he signed himself — wanted to be reappointed. His term expired at the end of 1821. He had made his bid for renewal in writing and addressed it to William Crawford, Secretary of the Treasury, the Georgian in the Cabinet, his patron. According to Adams,Crawford was "as wary as a Jesuit" in recommending any appointments. In this case he forwarded Morel's request, without comment, to Adams for consideration by the President.

The Secretary of State faithfully presented the letter to Monroe. He also reported that the Governor of Georgia, the President of the Georgia Senate, and the Speaker of the Georgia House — all known enemies of Crawford — had signed a memorial opposing the reappointment. The specific fitness of Morel as the President's delegate to safeguard the Africans in his care, and their dwindling number, Adams did not touch on, but he did mention an anonymous letter he had received which charged Morel with the "most atrocious" murder of a Negro. The Marshal, a white man, had been indicted for the crime; his subsequent acquittal did not remove the significance of the indictment by a grand jury of white Georgians.

The President said he believed there was too much truth in the anonymous letter. The President said that he wished to get rid of the man. Adams suggested that enemies of Crawford might be behind the accusation. Adams suggested that Crawford be asked if he recommended the reappointment. Crawford was Adams' enemy, too, and his political skills might also have been described as jesuitical.

The result of the mutual maneuvering was that not Crawford himself, but two of Crawford's friends, Congressmen Albert Cuthbert and Edward Tatnall, — one-sixth of the Georgia delegation in the House — did make the recommendation; Tatnall was also an old friend of Berrien. The President was given the choice of responding to the Crawford faction or being guided by his suspicion of Morel. He put the matter over, past January 1 and the expiration of the Marshal's term.

To his Diary, Adams confided his belief as to Morel that "the uneffaceable stain of blood was upon his hands." Like the President, he appeared to believe the allegation of murder was true or at least that Morel had killed a Negro. Before the appointment was decided, he received Habersham's letter announcing his appeal to the Supreme Court. From it he could infer that the Africans in Savannah would be in the Marshal's hands a new and indeterminate time while the appeal was processed. Adams did not bring this new aspect of the situation to the President. James Monroe reappointed John Morel.

Eleazar Early, Postmaster of Savannah, came to Washington in October 1822 with a story which he insisted on telling to Secretary of War Calhoun, a fellow Southerner, and then to the President himself. It concerned Morel's treatment of the Africans. It was circumstantial enough and from such a dispassionate and respectable source that the President felt bound to communicate it to the Cabinet. Adams summarized what the Cabinet was told:

> . . . the Marshal for the District of Georgia was now accumulating a fortune of at least thirty thousand a year by working a number of African negroes who are in his possession as Marshal of the District, while at the same time he is making the most enormous charges against the public for the maintenance of the very same negroes; that he makes it his open boast that he holds the office of Marshal for no other purpose, and that he intends to *swamp* the negroes — that is, to work them to death — before they shall be finally adjudicated out of his possession. Mr. Early adds that his cruelty to negroes is universally notorious, and that it is equally well known that he did commit the murder of the black man for which he was tried and acquitted. The principal witnesses against him were *spirited* away. Early declares himself to be of the same political party with the Marshal (Crawford's), but is so horror-struck at the character and conduct of the man that he feels it to be his duty to denounce him.

Early was afraid to accuse the Marshal in public. He asked the President to order the District Judge and the District Attorney to investigate.

Under federal law a marshal could be removed from office "at pleasure" of the President. Calhoun proposed that this marshal be removed instantly. The President said he could not remove him when no one had accused him publicly. The President thought he should stop payment on Morel's bills. The President thought that the District Attorney should be asked to investigate.

John Quincy Adams doubted that the President's plan would avail. Habersham "had shown that he was not the man to grapple with deep and deadly villainy supported by wealth and standing in society" — Adams meant that the District Attorney had tolerated the piratical federal customs collector Bullock, the son-in-law of a Georgia senator, against whom the President himself had been reluctant to proceed. Adams did not speak of Habersham's persistence in *The Antelope* against Judge Berrien, Judge Charlton, Judge Davies and Justice Johnson. He did not offer any alternative proposal to the President.

Monroe went ahead with the investigation. The time it took for him to give the order, for Habersham to make a report, and for the Administration to act upon it, must be inferred from three recorded events: Habersham was paid $431.75 by the Navy on December 27, 1823, as "compensation and expenses in the investigation made into the conduct of J.H. Morel, late Marshal of Georgia, in relation to the negroes of the cargo of the *General Ramirez.*" In June 1823 Morel submitted a bill to the Navy for expenses of $12,659, covering the period June 1, 1822 — May 30, 1823, and payment was denied. By the end of May 1823, almost all of the Africans were, by the Marshal's own account, no longer with him.

These facts suggest that Habersham conducted an investigation early in 1823 — say three months after the Cabinet's conversation — and that the Navy acted upon his report in the spring of 1823, concluding that the Marshal's conduct warranted removal of the Africans and refusal of his bill. The Marshal, however, was not indicted — the difficulty of securing witnesses against him would have been the reason, or the excuse.

Despite the reference in the Navy's accounts to "the late Marshal," he was not overtaken by death or removal from office. He remained ready to participate again in the case if there should be a need for his services. The appellants, for the time being at least, were moved to less bloodstained hands.

The Balance of the Attorney General.
September 1822 — February 1823

Men are by nature more conjugal than political animals, Aristotle once observed, a remark often neglected when his other aphorism about man as a political animal is recalled. Adams, a more political animal than most men, noted of William Wirt that he "appeared to think more about his salary, or what he called bread and meat for his children, than of any other subject." When he had been made chancellor in Virginia, an appointment which made him, a young man, the colleague of the legendary George Wythe, he had resigned after three years because, he said, at $1500 per year it was "a very empty thing, stomachically speaking." When he became Attorney General at $3000 a year, he stipulated with the President that he be allowed to keep his private practice. His salary was raised in 1819 to $3500, but by 1821 he was in debt to several banks, he was being charged ten percent on renewals of his loans, his liver bothered him, and he had ten living children. Three months after the apoplexy which had incapacitated him for work in the February term, Wirt was in Maryland seeking trial work for private clients. He obtained a retainer of $250 from the Bank of the United States and had the hope of trial fees from the Bank of $1500 to $2000. "[T]rial fees," he wrote his wife, "are the fees that *tell.*" In May his note of $1600 to a bank was called. "Suppose," he wrote his wife, that we were "dependent on salary. Only suppose it! Is it not then Heaven-directed that I have been able to leap into a practice which I believe will enable me to laugh at their demands?" It was his statutory duty "to prosecute and conduct all suits in the Supreme Court in which the United States shall be concerned"; but as he charged $500 apiece for every case in the Supreme Court in which he was not representing the United States, he had to weigh his statutory duty against his sense of obligation to his family.

Composing that balance as it bore on *The Antelope,* Wirt took into account the governing law as it emerged from *La Jeune Eugénie,* as it was applied by him to *La Pensée,* and as he again found it to be in the fall of 1822 when human liberty was put at issue. John Barry, owned by Mrs. Johnson of St. Croix, Virgin Islands, had been a stowaway on an American ship. When he was discovered in New York, the Danish Minister demanded his return as a Danish slave. Monroe consulted Wirt and was told that he had the power and the duty to hand John Barry over without trial. "I see no difference," Wirt wrote, "between the President's authority to restore this slave and his authority to restore a ship or any other property belonging to a subject of a foreign prince, which has been improperly taken from his possession by our citizens, or by force furnished from the United States." Wirt integrated the Act in Addition into this conclusion: the Act confirmed the President's power — its policy was "to avoid the increase of the number of blacks among us." Adams commented that Wirt's opinion arose from his "Virginia *Autocracy* against slaves," autocracy being used and underlined to express, in secret, Adams' detestation of the arrogance of slaveholders. But for Wirt the President's power was an evident corollary of the doctrine the President and Adams had forced on Story.

Once the opinion on John Barry had been issued by the Attorney General, in October 1822, with what conviction could he pursue the appeal of *The Antelope?* "Property" which had been "improperly taken" by "a force furnished from the United States" was an exact description of the Africans of the *Antelope* as seen by the Vice Consuls of Spain and Portugal. The purpose of the Act in Addition, as seen by the Attorney General, would be satisfied if the United States abandoned its appeal and the Spanish and Portuguese removed their slaves. Nothing was gained by winning and transporting the Africans to freedom, nothing, at any rate, which Wirt recognized as the intention of Congress.

Yet, as the legal doubts of the Attorney General increased, there was, perhaps, a change in the element of foreign policy in the Administration's balance. Portugal had been evidently weakened by the secession of Brazil in September 1822; Spain was not succeeding in retaking her rebellious colonies; and the most powerful of maritime nations, Great Britain, was pressing Portugal, Spain and the United States to extirpate the international slave trade. Adams did not cease to be conscious of the evils of slavery and, abstractly, he was the opponent of the slave trade. Stratford Canning, the new British minister to Washington, pressed upon him the British government's desire for joint action with the United States to end the trade, pointing out that only exercise of the right of search would end American participation under the cover of foreign flags. Adams replied by calling attention to the Act of May 15, 1820, making slave trading piracy. "This statute," he wrote, "makes every citizen of the United States concerned in such covered traffic liable, if detected in it, to suffer an ignominious death."

Adams did not remark that Captain John Smith had not suffered an ignominious death; nor did he observe that if a United States senator was concerned in the covered traffic, he was unlikely to be even questioned about it. Habersham had sent Adams a copy of Judge Davies' opinion in which a portion of the Africans on the *Antelope* were identified as slaves liberated from the *Exchange* of Bristol, Rhode Island, but no one in Washington had asked Barnabas Bates, the anti-slave trade Collector of Bristol, to find out who owned the *Exchange* or to initiate any kind of prosecution. Much less had anyone in Washington made the inquiries that would have led to the discovery that the *Rambler,* for whom the *Exchange* was tender, was owned by Senator James DeWolfe, a portion of whose own forfeitable property, it might then be guessed, was at stake in *The Antelope.* No one in Washington had had any appetite for linking the Senator from Rhode Island with a federal crime punishable by death.

The Colonization Society was in no position to urge the Administration to be more forceful in carrying out the Act in Addition by at least arguing *The Antelope* to the high Court. The Society had only acquired land at Cape Mesurado, West Africa at the end of December 1821. In November of 1822, the new colonists, mostly emancipated American Negroes and numbering no more than 130, were attacked by hostile tribes; seven men were killed, seven children were kidnapped. As the attacks continued into the spring of 1823, the Society's Agent advised the Secretary of the Navy on the special problem created by sending Africans from captured slavers: "There is much jealousy of the natives against them, for fear of their retaliation of their being sold. I would therefore respectfully recommend to Government not to send out any more captured Africans until the requisite buildings can be established and a regular establishment made for them."

No change had occurred in the domestic considerations which made the President and Adams willing to acquiesce in inaction — to the contrary. If 1822 had been a time for banking domestic fires, 1823 was a time for even greater caution. Justice Story who had been struck by the presidential politics of 1822 was categorical about 1823. "[T]he great business in Washington," he observed, "seems to be speculation as to the next President."

On February 7, 1823, Adams wrote the Attorney General at the President's direction about the *Apollon,* a French ship seized by the Treasury for evasion of tonnage duties. The case, which troubled relations with France, was on appeal from the federal courts in Georgia. *The Apollon,* Adams wrote Wirt, "should if possible be decided at the present session of the Supreme Court of the United States." No similar direction came from the President or the Secretary of State to argue *The Antelope* in 1823.

The Attorney General did argue eight cases in the Supreme Court for the United States. He also appeared as private counsel for a surveyor from Virginia, the city corporation of Washington and the purchaser of land from a Virginia trust. With this balance of public and private business kept, with the conviction that the policy of the Act in Addition was satisfied if Africans were kept out of the country, with Monroe and Adams avoiding every unnecessary inflammation of sentiment about slavery, and with the chief sponsors of African colonization beset, William Wirt did not argue *The Antelope;* and the order of the Supreme Court in the case in 1823, as in 1822, was "Continued."

The Case Abandoned. February — April 1824

If in 1822 the whole Cabinet was "by the ears" and all public business was "colored with hues borrowed from this subject," if in 1823 "the great business in Washington" was speculation as to the next President, what shall be said of the year in which the election would actually occur? The Administration had not the slightest incentive to bring *The Antelope* before the February 1824 Term of the Supreme Court. Wirt appeared five times for the United States. He also appeared for a landowner in Pennsylvania, the beneficiary of a testamentary trust in Maryland, a purchaser of tobacco in Maryland, a land claimant in Kentucky and the purchaser of glebe lands from the Episcopal Church of Alexandria, Virginia, increasing thereby his statutory income almost seventy-five percent. He did not appear for the Africans of the *Antelope,* and the order of the Court was, once more, "Continued."

Crawford, the one member of the Administration committed to the Act in Addition, was by now so sick that doubt existed as to whether he could sign his name as the Secretary of the Treasury.

When the Term was over in March, Wirt let it be known that the government would drop the case.

Paradoxical as it might appear, at the same time Adams was moving on the diplomatic front to restrict the slave trade. The past June, Stratford Canning had reported to London that Adams' political ambitions made an American-English agreement on the trade impossible. But Adams had surprised him by writing that if England made the slave trade piracy, the right to search would follow: "Piracy being an offense against the human race has its well-known incidents of capture and punishment by death by the peoples of tribunals of every country." With the change of classification, by this handy legal fiction, Adams' scruples about search disappeared. True, this solution had not occurred to Adams as a justification of the American taking of *La Jeune Eugénie.* True, the peremptory naval orders, forbidding American warships from searching foreign-flag vessels, were not revoked in obedience to Adams' new insight. But with apparent sincerity Adams advanced this thesis, inconsistent as it was with past and present Administration action. Classified as "pirates," slave traders became pursuable. It was, Adams explained, "the nature of the crime which draws after it the necessary consequences of capture and punishment."

Parliament followed Congress by changing "the nature of the crime." On March 13, 1824, the United States and Great Britain signed a Convention agreeing to suppress the trade as piracy and giving each other a mutual right of search. With this triumph, Adams had struck what seemed to him a resounding blow for human liberty. With this triumph, the Administration could let irritants like *The Antelope* sink from sight.

On April 12, Charles Harris and Thomas U.P. Charlton acknowledged payment "in full" for their services in Georgia, each receiving $300 in addition to the $600 they had divided from the sale of *The Antelope.* Their nominal client, Charles Mulvey, Vice Consul of Spain, had died of consumption, aged twenty-nine.

Payment was made on behalf of Cuesta Manzanal and Brother. Francis Sorrell, Vice Consul of Portugal, attested the payment and may well have been the straw through whom it was made. The amount owing Judge Berrien was yet to be determined; and Berrien, now preparing for his own election to the Senate, was informed that Wirt had abandoned the case. No purpose seemed served by its pursuit. The Attorney General, however, had not yet filed a motion to withdraw the appeal.

The Case Resurrected. May 1824 — February 1825

On May 22, 1824, the Senate gutted Adams' agreement with England. The day before, in a Special Message, Monroe had urged the necessity of action. But the Senate struck the provision permitting search of American ships off the coast of the United States. With this deletion the treaty became unacceptable to England, and Adams' chosen way of restraining the slave trade was dead. In these circumstances *The Antelope* was no longer only an irritant to the Administration; it was the tangible sign of any Administration activity against the slave trade. The decision to pick up the case was made against the background of Adams' defeat.

According to Berrien, a member of the Colonization Society persuaded Wirt not to abandon the case. The Society was now ready for the Africans. Peace had come to its colony in 1824. In August of that year the Society's Agent promulgated laws for what was now described as Liberia. Three hundred and eight black colonists had arrived. Obtaining the Africans of the *Antelope* could be seen as a way of rapidly augmenting the population. The objective conditions for receiving them existed. The member who acted for the Society was in all probability Francis Scott Key.

Not only had Key taken the lead in 1819 in lobbying with Wirt on the meaning of the Act in Addition, but in 1824 he served as co-counsel with him in two cases, that of the slaver *Merino*, where

Wirt invited him to act for the United States, and the private case of the glebe lands of the Episcopal Church, where his knowledge of matters Episcopalian was of special value. He had access to the Attorney General and the Attorney General's good will. He also had motivation. Always devout, always humanitarian and anxious to stop the slave trade, Key had reacted to the drowning of his eight-year-old son Edward in the Potomac, in 1822, with a special dedication of himself: henceforth, he would be no longer "a slave of the world," but a "servant of God." He acted, he believed, not for himself, but for Christ, whose "felt presence was my strength." With new religious dedication he acted against the slave trade. That he was, coincidentally, the first cousin of the counsel for the Spanish Vice Consul, Thomas U.P. Charlton, did not decrease his zeal for the Africans he sought to save. The Colonization Society had been and remained his prime philanthropic endeavor.

Key might persuade Wirt not to give up, but who could make Wirt go forward? In the summer of 1824 Key gave his views on how the Administration operated and what would move it, when his cousin asked his help in being appointed Minister to Mexico. His comic scenario was as follows. After referring to the recommendations he had received for others, the President would say:

> But Sir as to Mr. Charlton you may assure him that there can be no such thing as overlooking the pretensions of such a man. And, to be candid Sir, I will express to you my sincere hope that when the matter comes up before us Mr. Charlton's services & standing may be duly estimated, & that it may be in our power to gratify our wishes in regard to him.

On that imaginary conversation, Key commented:

> Now if you can find out from this what your chance is, you are far more quick-sighted than our Court followers here, who have been studying such answers for years without being able to make anything of them yet.

What would move Mr. Adams, the lynchpin of the Administration?

> That would depend entirely upon the person that called upon him. If he was a man that could turn a state or perhaps even a county on the presidential question, the Secretary would try to bend his stiff sinews & soften his hard face, & would be as polite & promising as possible, & would look more smooth than it could be thought such a cross-grained piece of stuff ever could.

Having made that acute analysis for Charlton, and knowing he himself rated as "but a Cypher" with Adams, Key knew what it would take to bring *The Antelope* before the Supreme Court.

In the November election, the battle between Adams, Clay, Crawford and Jackson — "The War of the Giants" — ended without a majority for any of them; or rather, did not end, but entered a more frenetic stage, with Clay virtually eliminated, Crawford hurt and Jackson, with a plurality, locked in combat with Adams. Victory was to be awarded in February by the House of Representatives, in a ballot in which each state would have one vote and each state's vote would be determined by a majority of its Congressmen, so that small states became as important as big states, and in divided delegations each Congressman became a President-maker. "Bargain" — the term applied by Jacksonites to the understanding by which Henry Clay became Adams' Secretary of State and Adams received the votes of Clay's supporters — is too crude and commercial a term to convey the kind of understanding by which experienced politicians let each other know that expectations might be mutually satisfied by the Congressmen and the President-elect. In this exchange, electioneering was — Adams' phrase — "kindling into fury." At the center or the blaze, not proof against it, was Adams himself.

All Adams' diplomacy had not changed the perception of him in a city like Savannah. He was "the bitterest Federalist in Heart

& Soul in America." He was "a Monk . . . an Inquisitor . . . still a School Master . . ." who "might do in Portugal" but who was "totally unfit for the head of this nation." Such was his description by Charles Harris, who, though having appeared for interests in *The Antelope* labeled Portuguese and Spanish, still thought of these Latin nations as representing all that was odious to a true Anglo-Saxon believer in liberty. Adams could not hope to change this kind of southern response to his ill-concealed righteousness. He still had hopes in the border states.

Maryland was a state whose vote was undecided and therefore critical. Nine members composed the delegation. Three congressmen for Adams plus two for Clay gave Adams a majority of one in Maryland if the friends of Clay followed his lead. Adams wooed the delegation in person.

Isaac McKim was a member of the Maryland congressional delegation from Baltimore. He was also a Vice President of the Colonization Society. In the first year of the Society's existence he had subscribed $500 to the Society, sixteen times as much as Francis Scott Key, five times as much as Bushrod Washington, and over twice as much as anyone else. It may not be unreasonable to measure his interest in the Society's affairs by the money he was willing to pledge on its behalf. Although on second thought he reduced his subscription to $250, he stood out as its chief philanthropist.

On January 15 and January 21, Isaac McKim called on John Quincy Adams. According to Adams' Diary, the purpose of the visit on January 15 was to introduce a friend with a claim against Spain "from the Habanna"; the purpose of the visit on January 21 was to read to the Secretary of State a letter from a constituent in Baltimore touching claims against the Netherlands. If a Congressman from Baltimore called twice within a week on the leading candidate for the presidency, it must be a matter of speculation as to whether other topics of interest to the Congressman were mentioned; it may be a legitimate inference that they were.

By a majority of one Congressman, Maryland voted for John Quincy Adams. By a majority of one state, Adams was elected President on February 9, on the first ballot in the House of Representatives.

On February 19 the annual meeting of the Colonization Society was held in Washington in the Capitol, in the Supreme Court Room. Several justices of the Supreme Court were in attendance. The meeting was addressed by Lieutenant Stockton, commander of the *Alligator* and captor of *La Jeune Eugénie,* and by the Reverend Ralph Gurley, the new Executive Secretary of the Society. Lieutenant Stockton asked his audience to consider Spain, reduced by the King of Kings to wretchedness on account of the crimes of Spaniards against the unoffending natives of America and Africa. He prayed that the United States would not perish of a heart ossified by countless cruelties to the Indian and the African. Ralph Gurley declared that the slave trade was denounced by all Christian nations. He trusted that no efforts would be spared to reach the public mind on the objects of the Society and "through this to reach those Higher Powers, upon which depend the success of our operations, which alone carry on to a completion this great work." The Higher Powers which Gurley hoped to reach by public opinion could not have been supernatural. The powers he had in mind must have been those in charge of the government of the United States. Ten days after the election, the Society was sure that those Higher Powers had approved its case.

On February 26, one week after the annual meeting, less than two weeks after the election, *The Antelope,* stranded in the Supreme Court for just three years, was argued to the Court. It was argued by William Wirt — Adams' designate to carry on as Attorney General — and by Francis Scott Key. The argument went on for five days and drew large audiences to the Supreme Court Room in the basement of the Capitol. The climax, when all four counsel summed up, came Thursday, March 3, the eve of Adams' Inauguration.

· 6 ·

Supreme Law

An Uncommon Excitement.
February 26 — March 3, 1825

At high noon, Saturday, February 26, Francis Scott Key opened for the United States in the Supreme Court of the United States the argument for the Africans of the *Antelope.* Key had been a member of the Supreme Court bar since he was twenty-seven years of age; he was now forty-five. No other lawyer in the case had been so long an advocate before the Court. In 42 appearances, he had won 18 times, lost 23 times and had a mixed result or tie once; counting the tie as a nullity, his average was .439.

Key had not always appeared on the side of human liberty. In 1812, in *Wood v. Davis,* he had argued successfully for Wood, who claimed he was not bound by a judgment that the mother of Davis was free. Four years later, in *Negro John Davis v. Wood,* he defeated a second attempt of Davis to gain his freedom. In 1810, however, in *Scott v. Negro Ben,* he had represented Ben, and in *Sally Henry v. Ball* he had represented Sally Henry, each time trying to show that a slave was actually a free person. In 1812, in *Mima Queen and Child v. Hepburn,* a case that was to have a bearing on the decision of *The Antelope,* he had acted for Mima

Queen and her child. He had lost for Ben, Sally Henry and Mima Queen and her child, so that his average in winning human freedom was .000.

On the same side, closing for the United States and the Africans, was William Wirt. Before becoming Attorney General he had argued only twice in the Supreme Court, but since his appointment he had appeared in approximately 70 cases, about two-thirds of them for the United States or its officers and about one-third for private clients. Overall, he had won 39 times, lost 29 times, and tied twice, for an average of .574.

In the 1820 Term Wirt had won *La Josefa Segunda,* the case of the Venezuelan privateer cited by Judge Davies in the District Court. On behalf of the United States Wirt had successfully contended that the privateer — not shown to have been in breach of the American neutrality law — had acquired title to the Spanish slaves she had seized; when she tried to run them into New Orleans, the United States was justified in holding them forfeit, however innocent the original Spanish owner. He had lost *The Bello Corrunes* in the 1821 Term where he had argued that a Spanish vice consul had no authority to speak for individual Spanish property owners, and Justice Johnson had written that a vice consul might assert the rights of nationals of his country wherever "the "vicissitudes of human affairs may force them." In the same year he had successfully appeared in *La Concepcion* for a Spanish vice consul in a suit against a privateer commissioned by the revolutionary government of Buenos Aires. In the 1823 Term he had lost *The Mary Ann* where he attempted to sustain the forfeiture of a slaver to the government. In the 1824 Term he had won *The St. Iago de Cuba,* where Justice Story agreed with him that a slaver "colorably a Spaniard, was really an American," and *The Margaret alias Carlos Fernando,* where he showed that the registration of a ship as Spanish was a fraud committed by the American owners. Together with Key he obtained a mixed result in *The Merino,* another slaver, with owners based in Cuba claiming to be Spanish. With this substantial experience in penetrating marine fraud, with this practical knowledge of the ways of American slave traders and with this formidable recent experience in advocacy before the Court, Wirt was the most accomplished of counsel in the case.

On behalf of the Vice Consul of Spain, John Macpherson Berrien opposed Key and the Attorney General. No longer a Georgia judge, Berrien had been elected United States Senator from Georgia in November 1824 and was due to take office on March 3, 1825. He came before the Court not as a veteran of the small Supreme Court bar — his record, all in cases argued in the 1818 Term, stood at two wins, one tie, an average of 1.000 — but as Senator-elect and the lawyer who had shaped the case since it began on July 15, 1820, in Judge Davies' court in Savannah.

With him was Charles Jared Ingersoll, who spoke in the name of the Vice Consul of the King of Portugal. Ingersoll, a former congressman and a former chairman of the House Judiciary Committee, had been talked of as Attorney General in 1817 at the time Wirt was appointed. A friendly observer noted that he would have been a "monstrous fool to go to Washington" when in Philadelphia he was "rapidly accumulating a fortune." He accepted appointment by Monroe as District Attorney for the Eastern District of Pennsylvania, an office he could combine with the practice of law in Philadelphia. In fifteen appearances before the Supreme Court, he had won 8 times, lost 6, and tied once for an average of .571. He had represented one revolutionary privateer successfully in *La Amistad de Rues,* and another unsuccessfully in *The Estrella.* He had been defeated by Wirt in *La Josefa Segunda,* where he had been the lawyer for the Spanish slave-owner. He had half won, half lost against Key and Wirt in *The Merino* the year before. Next to Wirt, he was the lawyer in the case most familiar with the law of the sea as it affected privateers and slavers.

The lawyers, in short, had had considerable experience on the several sides of the issues before the Court. Key had represented slave-owners. Wirt, between the decision in *La Jeune Eugénie* and his argument in *The Antelope,* had been unsympathetic to the Africans. Ingersoll had acted against the colonial powers in Latin America. Berrien had shifted from representing the captain of the Treasury cutter to representing a claimant of the goods. Counsel were not unevenly matched: Berrien and Ingersoll held a slight statistical advantage; no one could rival Berrien in familiarity with the facts of the case; Key and Wirt were unsurpassed in knowledge of the judges.

Key opened on Saturday, Berrien spoke on Monday, Ingersoll on Tuesday, Wirt on Wednesday, and all four engaged in the reprise on Inauguration Eve. Our opponents, Berrien wrote Charles Harris the day after the argument was over, "certainly have the advantage of a prevailing mania on the subject of slavery, which has reached the Bench. The discussion of this case has provided an uncommon excitement . . ." Wirt's closing argument was "worthy of all praise" — such was the admiration drawn from a Boston newspaper and nationally reported by *Niles Weekly Register.* Henry Foote, later Senator from Mississippi, recorded that a packed gallery of gentlemen and ladies was held enraptured by Berrien's "distinct, sonorous and impressive" voice. Yet the audience was still more moved by the argument made by Key. The case had "enlisted in a splendid manner the generous sensitivities of his soul." He "closed with a thrilling and even electrifying picture of the horrors connected with the African Slave Trade which would have done honor to a Pitt or a Wilberforce in their palmiest days."

Key began with the least controversial reason for the Act in Addition, the one William Wirt had always believed in — the Act was a response to a specific demographic danger. "Our national policy," he declared, "perhaps our national safety, requires that there be no increase in this species of population within our territory." The prohibition against the importation of Africans and the requirement that, if imported, they be removed were absolute. It did not matter what the intention of the original owners, be they Spanish or Portuguese, had been. The Africans of the *Antelope* had been in the course of importation, contrary to the absolute prohibition. By force of the statute alone, they had been liberated when they came within reach of American law.

If the statutory law did not impose liability on the slave-owners and confer liberty on the slaves irrespective of intent, Key had a second argument which was both technical and humane. He appealed to the rules of evidence in the context of the case:

> . . . those human beings, who are claimed as property, come into the jurisdiction of the court not by any wrongful act of ours, but lawfully, profidentially; and are to be treated just as if they were thrown upon our shore by a storm. The Spanish owners show, as proof of property, their previous possession; and the possessor of goods, it is said, is to be presumed the lawful owner. This is true as to *goods*, because they have universally and necessarily an owner. But these are *men*, of whom it cannot be affirmed, that they have universally and necessarily an owner. In some particular and excepted cases, depending upon the local law and usage, they may be the subjects of property and ownership; but by the law of nature, all men are free. The presumption that even black men and Africans are slaves, is not a universal presumption. It would be manifestly unjust to throw the *onus probandi* upon them, to prove their birthright.

What must the Spanish and Portuguese do to sustain their burden of proof? It was not enough to establish that they had a title locally recognized. They must show that the law of nations required the recognition of their title by an American court. Suppose, said Key, that these men instead of being Africans were Europeans rescued by an American warship from an Algerian corsair off the Barbary Coast. Could the Vice Consul of the Bey of Algiers reclaim them in an American court because they were slaves under the law of Barbary? The Vice Consuls of Spain and Portugal here must show that the law of nations compelled an American court to uphold property in persons.

Did the law of nations sanction ownership acquired in the slave trade? If it ever had, it was when the trade "consisted merely in the transportation of persons who were slaves in Africa, to be slaves elsewhere." Circumstances had changed the character of the trade and led to its general reprobation. "Slaves are no longer acquired, merely by capture in war or by trade; but free persons are seized and carried off by the traders and their agents. Wars are instigated by them for the mere purpose of making slaves. The persons thus enslaved are clandestinely brought away, under circumstances of extreme cruelty, aggravated by the necessity of concealment, and smuggled into every country where the cupidity of avarice creates a demand for these unhappy victims." International law had evolved. It now condemned the slave trade. A slaver had no right now acknowledged by the law of nations to ask judicial aid in the recovery of his human property.

Beyond a title which an American court was bound to honor, the claimants must show that they were in fact the owners. The Vice Consul of Portugal had not shown that there were any particular Portuguese claiming these persons. A mere showing that some Africans came from ships flying Portuguese colors was no proof that subjects of Portugal had owned either the ships or the Africans. The names of the supposed Portuguese owners had never been disclosed. Did such owners exist? Their right to any property was unproven as long as their existence was unproven.

The identity of the slaves claimed was equally unestablished. Neither the Vice Consul of Portugal nor the Vice Consul of Spain had shown which particular Africans were theirs. A lottery was not a substitute for proof. At stake was human liberty. The slave traders could not use the lot to take as property human beings whom they could not identify as individual persons.

No reader of the Christian Gospels — certainly no reader who was as convinced a believer as Key — could have spoken of the lottery of which the Africans were the subjects without an echo in his heart of that other lottery following the Crucifixion in St. John. The memory of that last indignity of the Passion would have brought together in his mind that innocent victim of the law whom Christians worship and the innocent victims of the law whom Key was befriending.

Beginning with an argument of statutory construction that undercut all contention over ownership by invoking absolute liability, Key had put his best argument last. A lottery was not a way of proving human identity. In between he had hit at the weakest point in the Portuguese case, and he had adapted Story's critique of the international status of the slave trade — the burning language of *La Jeune Eugénie* lived again — and tied these arguments to his strong technical position that the burden of proof of title rested with the slave traders. A stronger case could not have been made.

Replying, Senator Berrien also began on a technical note. The United States had acquired possession of the *Antelope* illegally: Captain Jackson had no authority under the revenue laws to intercept a slaver. The President had authority under the Act in Addition, but the President had never given instructions to Captain Jackson. If he had lost his vessel in his chase of the *Antelope*, could he have justified himself in a court-martial? John Jackson, Berrien said, speaking of his first client in the case, had abandoned his duty and left the limits entrusted to his vigilance. His taking had been lawless.

Assuming, however, that the capture was legal, could the United States penalize the foreigners whose property had against their will been brought within range of an American revenue cutter? "Subjects of Spain and Portugal" had been "quietly pursuing this traffic under the sanction of their own laws." They should not be deprived of their goods because a pirate had brought them to a country which disapproved of their practice.

By the treaty of San Lorenzo el Real, the United States was bound to make restitution of Spanish property taken by pirates.

His opponent, Senator Berrien suggested, was asking the Court to hold the slave trade illegal because it was immoral. Morality and law were, however, distinct. Senator Berrien asked the Court to enforce the law:

> [W]ould it become the United States to assume to themselves the character of censors of the morals of the world on this subject? To realize the lofty conception of the adverse counsel, and consider themselves as the ministers of Heaven, called to wipe out from among the nations the stain of this iniquity? Might not the foreign claimant thus rebuke them, in the strong language of truth? For more than thirty years you were slave traders; you are still extensively slaveowners. If the slave-trade be robbery, you were robbers, and are yet clinging to your plunder. For more than twenty years, this traffic was protected by your constitution, exempted from the whole force of your legislative power; its fruits yet lie at the foundation of that compact. The principle by which you continue to enjoy them is protected by that constitution, forms a basis for your representatives, is infused into your laws, and mingles itself with all the sources of authority. Relieve yourself from these absurdities before you assume the right of sitting in judgment on the morality of other nations. But this you cannot do. Paradoxical as it may appear, they constitute the very bond of your union. The shield of your constitution protects them from your touch.
>
> We have no pretense, then, to enforce against others our own peculiar notions of morality. The standard of morality, by which courts of justice must be guided, is that which the law prescribes.

Was the slave trade of Spanish and Portuguese citizens in Africa contrary to the law? Not to American law, which operated only on American subjects or on aliens within American jurisdiction. Was it contrary, then, to international law? That question, Senator Berrien said, was linked to another: Was slavery contrary to the law of nations? Slavery had existed from time immemorial. The transportation of slaves between two countries was only an incident to the basic institution. To show the slave trade condemned by international law, one must show that slavery was so condemned. "If humanity nerves the arm of the law, why is its force spent on the incident? Why is it powerless in relation to the principal wrong?" The question pointed to a *reductio ad absurdum.* No one, Senator Berrien assumed, would contend that the law of nations made domestic slavery illegal when by that standard the slave system of the United States itself would be illegal.

La Jeune Eugénie was the only American case teaching that the slave trade was against international law. The learned judge who decided that case had found the slave trade to be condemned for its inhumanity. Were murder and robbery, also inhumane acts, then condemned by international law? The learned judge had said that the slave trade was contrary to some of the first principles which ought to govern nations. Smuggling, too, was contrary to some first principles — it began in perjury, violated civic duty, sometimes even [illegible]ted in murder. Could smuggling, asked Senator Berrien, be punished under the law of nations?

La Jeune Eugénie was a curious case for the appellant to rely on. The learned judge had said the trade was illegal, but he had acceded to the suggestion of the State Department that the ship be turned over to the Vice Consul of France. Would his adversaries, Senator Berrien inquired, care to observe that precedent and surrender the property at issue here to the consular agents of Spain and Portugal?

The matter of the lottery was taken up in a pause in Berrien's analysis of "the great issue," the legality of slave-trading. A lottery was a proper way to distribute property which consisted in an undividided interest or undifferentiated mass. The Negroes had been "ascertained" to be property. As property they were an undivided mass which must be distributed in shares by some convenient method. To make the division by lot was a sensible approach. The United States had no standing to attack the means chosen. The District Attorney had participated in the lottery. He had availed himself of it to identify the Africans from the American vessel. The United States could not now disown the acceptance of the lottery by its representative.

Berrien had met Key's attack on the lottery with the invocation of a technical doctrine, estoppel. He had countered Key's construction of the Act in Addition by looking at another question of statutory meaning, the powers given to revenue cutters to enforce the Act. He had tried as hard as he could to make the whole case turn on the legality of the slave trade in international law. At the heart of his argument were two interlocking propositions: Law is not morals. The Constitution has sanctioned slavery. If law were a matter of morals, then the Court would have to face the morality of a basic constitutional institution. If law and morals were rigorously separated, the Constitution was safe from the application of any higher criterion, slavery was exempt from legal criticism, and the slave trade gave good title wherever local law made the slave trade legal.

Charles Jared Ingersoll, the Philadelphia lawyer, argued: If an African were found in a state of the Union permitting slavery, it would be presumed that he was a slave. The same must be true of an African found on a Spanish or Portuguese ship engaged in the slave trade in an area open to the slave trade under the laws of Spain and Portugal. The presumption had not been refuted. The property could not be lost by capture when the captor was a ship equipped in an American port in violation of the Neutrality Act.

As to what he also saw as the great issue, the law of nations was an unwritten "body of political ethics applied to nations." The law of nations was discovered in the fundamental treatises of writers on the subject, in judicial precedents, and in long usage. Recent judicial precedents, especially in England, were no doubt mixed and contradictory. But not a single treatise writer had been cited who taught that the slave trade was against the law of nations. Universal and immemorial usage showed the acceptance of the trade. Only in modern times, and then by specific statutes or treaties, had any nation outlawed the practice. The Court was now being asked "to anticipate, by judicial legislation" what could only be done by Congress and the President in the exercise of the treaty-making power. No warrant existed for the Court to announce a new law of nations and on its own authority decide that the slave trade was barred by international law.

William Wirt, Attorney General of the United States, began with the contention first made by Richard Wylly Habersham, which no judge in the lower courts had recognized: The Africans themselves were "parties to the cause." At least, said William Wirt, such of them as were free were parties to the cause. Supposing that the United States had made no case, he said, supposing that all the other parties to the proceeding had colluded, the Africans would still be entitled to the protection of the Court.

The Attorney General turned to Senator Berrien's contention that the *Dallas,* had acted lawlessly. The slave trade law of 1808, he said, was authority enough for a revenue cutter to seize any ship hovering off the coast of the United States for the purpose of selling or landing slaves. The Act of May 15, 1820, he added, made slave-trading piracy when carried on by an American citizen. The *Dallas* was fully authorized to enforce the statutes against piracy.

Lawfully brought into the country by the *Dallas,* what was the status of the Africans? They were free, unless proved to be slaves. *Habeas corpus* had been the form of the action in *Somerset's Case* over half a century before, in which Lord Mansfield had ruled that English air was too pure for slavery to exist in England. By implication Wirt called to mind this most famous of all Anglo-American freedom cases:

> The Africans stand before the court, as if brought up before it upon a *habeas corpus.* Suppose them here, on such a process, asserting their freedom, and claiming your protection; what kind of proof would

> you exact from those who claim to hold them in slavery? Most certainly, you would not demand inferior evidence to that which you require in a case of life or death. The witnesses must present themselves fairly before you. Their statements must be clear and consistent, and such as to command the confidence of the court. They must be sustained by the documentary evidence; and where any doubt is left, the decision should be *in favorem libertatis.*
>
> The claimants wish the court to consider this as a question exclusively between Spain on one side, and the United States on the other, in which these persons are to be considered as "effects," and "merchandise," taken by the pirates, and as such liable to restitution under the stipulations of the treaty of 1795. But is the court at liberty so to consider them, under the laws of our own country? Some of them are confessedly free, because the decree has established the fact. Which of them are slaves, it is impossible to determine, by any rule of evidence known to our practice. The claimants must prove their property; and this involves the necessity of proving that these persons are property. They must prove that they are property, and that they are *their* property.

Was naked possession of an African proof of ownership? the Attorney General asked. He did not think so. The natives of Africa were as free as the natives of Spain or Portugal. The Spanish and Portuguese slave traders must show their right to enslave them. Custom was insufficient. No right could grow out of the violation of justice and humanity. The existence of slavery in the United States was no "excuse or palliation for perpetuating and extending the guilt and misery of the slave trade."

Suppose, Wirt continued, that these persons were property under Spanish law. The United States had no obligation to apply Spanish law in its own courts. It would not do so in the case of a political crime. The obligation in the treaty with Spain to deliver up merchandise did not commit the United States to accept a Spanish definition of what constituted merchandise. The Africans were before the Court as persons. Under the law of the United States they were free persons.

Judgment Day. March 16, 1825

Seven justices constituted the Court. Justice Todd was sick and did not hear the case. How might the others — Marshall, Washington, Johnson, Duvall, Story and Thompson — be expected to vote? It was certain that William Johnson would support the decrees which he had issued in 1821 in Milledgeville and Savannah. It was probable that Joseph Story would be hostile to slave traders suing for property in a court of the United States, although, after bowing to the Administration's pressure in *La Jeune Eugénie*, he had shown anxiety about his colleagues' reaction to his surviving dicta. "I dare say you will think me a bold Judge," he wrote Bushrod Washington, describing his opinion as "très recherché" — a remarkably disarming characterization of his strong comments on slave traders. "Be it so," he continued, "but I must ask your patience to read before you condemn me. . . . You will find my opinion guarded and sober on all the ticklish points. I have not meddled at all with the question of the right of slavery in general, nor could I with any decent respect for the institutions of my country deem it proper to engage in such speculations." In this fashion Story anticipated Berrien's argument that to say B, one must say A. If this was the hesitant voice of a Northern liberal, how would the other four go?

The Chief Justice had been initially responsive to Story's dicta — "he thinks I am right, but the questions are new to his mind," Story wrote in February 1822; and Marshall's general commitment to the Colonization Society was old and strong He had made a special trip from Richmond to Washington to participate in the meeting which had formed the Colonization Society in December 1816. He had participated in the founding of the Richmond-Manchester Auxiliary of the Society in November 1823, and accepted election as its President. He had attended the national society's meeting in the Supreme Court room on February 19, 1825, and been elected a national vice president. He had listened to Lieutenant Stockton's oration on the divine judgment upon Spain and the danger of ossifying the American heart by cruelties to the African. He had heard the Reverend Gurley direct his appeal to the Higher Powers in the land.

There was, however, no guarantee that he had continued to agree with Story, if Story stayed firm, or that he would put his devotion to the Society above his vision of the law. The Chief Justice's vision of the law was of a special universe composed of rules. Like ministers, judges performed a communal rite discerning, enunciating and applying the principles which animated the rules. The intrusion of prejudice, of feeling, of personality into that sacred task was a form of sacrilege. The interest of the Colonization Society, the plight of the individual Africans, would weigh as nothing when he sought to divine the rules to decide *The Antelope.* That feeling should point in one direction could be reason to repress it.

In *Mima Queen and Child,* thirteen years before, Francis Scott Key had argued that to prove freedom, hearsay was admissible: a witness might testify as to what his mother had heard her father say about Mima Queen's ancestor. The Chief Justice had ruled that, as hearsay, the testimony should not be heard in court. "However the feelings of the individual may be interested on the part of a person claiming freedom" — the fatal dependent clause apology — Marshall could not see that these feelings were a basis for changing the rules. A case for freedom, he wrote, was not different from "general cases, in which a right to property may be asserted." The judgment that Mima Queen and her child were slaves was affirmed. The Chief Justice distinguished his feelings as an individual from his vision of the law.

In *The Antelope* Marshall had shown no uneasiness at the long delay in the government's presenting its case. At the close of 1824 he wrote James Monroe a note on his conduct of the presidency: "You may look back with pleasure to several very interesting events which have taken place during your administration, and have the rare felicity not to find the retrospect darkened by a single spot the review of which ought to pain yourself or your fellow citizens." *The Antelope* apparently did not count as an interesting event or dark spot. Nothing in its handling made the Chief Justice qualify his praise.

Bushrod Washington was still the President of the Colonization Society and, according to Story, was like Key "deeply and earnestly" committed to its goals. He was also a Virginian, a slave-owner and a lawyer committed to the concept that slaves were property. How would he take Berrien's argument that the slave trade could not be made internationally illegal without drawing into question the domestic institution? In the fall of 1821, Bushrod, the heir of George Washington, had sold 54 slaves from Mount Vernon to purchasers from the Red River, Louisiana. Some of those sold were separated from their husbands, others from their children. To newspaper criticism of his inhumanity, Bushrod Washington replied with an open letter denouncing "any person questioning our right, *legal or moral,* to dispose of property secured us by sanctions equally valid with those by which we hold every other species of property." The italics defending domestic slave trading were Bushrod Washington's. The equation between slaves and other species of property was his. If the issue were conceived by him as turning on title to property, he would be with Johnson.

Gabriel Duvall had the smallest reputation of the judges. He had been transferred in 1811 from Comptroller of the Currency to Justice of the Supreme Court. In fourteen years he had written only nine opinions and one dissent, a record of prodigious inactivity. Duvall was the judge whom John Quincy Adams had characterized in 1819 as feeble and inefficient in dealing with the privateers of Baltimore; he was now seventy-two years old and deaf.

In 1812, his first year on the Court, in *Wood v. Davis,* Duvall had stated in open court that when he had been in practice in Maryland he had filed petitions to establish freedom for "the Shorters, the Thomases, the Bostons, and many others," and he had proved their freedom by tracing their ancestry up to a free white woman. After judgment in those cases, he declared, the descendants of the petitioners had only to cite the judgment and prove their descent. Marshall, however, following the argument of Francis Scott Key for the slave-owner, adopted the contrary rule and permitted an owner to claim a child whose mother had been judged free. Duvall did not dissent. But in the same year he was moved to write the only dissenting opinion he was to author, and the question he addressed was what was needed to prove freedom. Against Marshall and the whole Court in *Mima Queen and Child,* he would have permitted the hearsay which Key had sought to introduce to prove the freedom of the petitioners.

"People of color," Duvall then wrote, "from their helpless condition, under the uncontrolled authority of a master, are entitled to all reasonable protection. A decision that hearsay evidence, in such cases, shall not be admitted, cuts up by the roots all claims of the kind, and puts a final end to them . . ." Hearsay to prove freedom was different from hearsay to prove the boundary of property. "It will universally be admitted," Duvall declared to his unheeding brethren, "that the right to freedom is more important than the right of property." He expressed a conviction bred in practice on behalf of the Shorters, Thomases and Bostons of Maryland. Would it carry over thirteen years later when the claimants were natives of Africa?

The most recent appointee, Smith Thompson, had consented to appointment by Monroe in 1823 only when he was sure he would not be nominated for President. He still harbored political ambitions. A New Yorker, he had taken the slave states' side in the Cabinet discussion of the Missouri bill in 1820. Yet in 1823, in dealing with *La Jeune Eugénie,* he had opposed the President's intervention in Story's court. When the British had proposed a reciprocal right of search as an essential step in suppressing the slave trade — a right Adams described as "more formidable to human liberty than the slave trade itself" — he had stood out in the Administration in support of the proposal. As Secretary of the Navy he had not been attentive to the Africans in Savannah, but he had been responsible for their maintenance. On the whole it might be guessed that he would stand with Story now.

If personal relations between the justices were to count for anything, Marshall, Washington and Story were bound by friendship, and they were alienated from Johnson. Duvall normally followed the Chief; Thompson was too new to have made any firm alliances. An observer predicting on the basis of their public identification with the Colonization Society would have counted Marshall and Washington with Story and Thompson for a vote of four to two in favor of the Africans. An observer predicting on the basis of crude sectional and property lines would have counted four Southerners and slave-owners to two Northerners and non-owners and guessed that the slave-owners would not hold the slave trade condemned by international law. No crude instrument, however, could have detected how the Court would go on the proof of the slaves' identity. No mechanical gauge could have predicted how stubbornly the feeble Gabriel Duvall might distinguish between rights of different importance to the person.

After argument and the Inauguration, two weeks remained in the February Term, of which one-sixth of the hearing time had already been directed to *The Antelope.* The large question of whether the international slave trade was internationally lawful had been on the Justices' horizon since 1821. If the Africans had had to wait three years for the Court to hear their case, it was now to be decided, along with more than a dozen more, in the next ten days. *Niles Weekly Register* remarked with emphasis, "This would seem to be doing business *fast enough.*"

The two Justices closest to the issues in *The Antelope* were doing much of the other work of the Court. While Duvall did not write, Thompson wrote once and Washington twice, Johnson was the author of five opinions and one dissent, and Story delivered six opinions. Johnson gave the opinion of the Court in favor of James DeWolfe in a case not involving slavery, but DeWolfe's business interests in Kentucky, where Henry Clay had once been his counsel. DeWolfe's connection to the *Antelope* through the *Rambler* of Bristol was not adverted to by the Court. The whole "Rhode Island connection" which the presence of the *Exchange* in the case made palpable was not one the United States had cared to explore.

The "most important judgment" of the year for Story was *Bank of the United States v. Bank of Georgia* where the issue was which of two banks bore the ultimate loss on a forged note, and Senator Berrien was the losing counsel. Story also wrote the opinion upholding the condemnation of the *Plattsburgh,* an American slaver equipped with false documents and a paper captain in Cuba, and the opinion apportioning the proceeds from the sale of *La Josefa Segunda,* the slaver whose condemnation had been sustained in the 1820 Term. As *La Josefa Segunda* had been captured before enactment of the Act in Addition, and as the Monroe Administration in the meeting at Adams' office on April 2, 1819, had decided not to apply the Act retrospectively, the 300 Africans aboard her had been auctioned. The Court was asked to decide who was entitled to the cash from the sale. Story held for the Collector of New Orleans, represented by the Attorney General. Key represented the losing revenue inspectors.

The Chief Justice wrote ten opinions: on a prize dispute from the War of 1812; on a piracy case; on a point of federal practice; on three questions of land in Kentucky and one of land in Tennessee; on two matters involving "the National," a lottery sponsored by the City of Washington with a grand prize of $100,000 in cash; and in *The Antelope,* where the lottery ordered by Justice

Johnson had distributed over $60,000 worth of human beings.

In the case at bar, the Chief Justice began, "the sacred rights of liberty and property come in conflict with each other." The Court "must not yield to feelings which might seduce it from the path of duty, and must obey the mandate of the law." In this introductory contrast of feelings and the law, the resolution of the status of the slave trade was forecast.

The trade had the sanction of long usage protected by the laws of the civilized nations of the world. "However abhorrent this traffic may be to a mind whose original feelings are not blunted by familiarity with the practice" — the classic dependent clause disavowed by the principal predicate was employed — the trade had been engaged in "as common commercial business" by all the nations with colonies. As "feelings of justice and humanity" gained ascendancy, it had been forbidden by statute, first by most individual states of the Union (Marshall wanted to show that America had led the way), then by Great Britain. The utmost efforts of Great Britain and the United States were now engaged in repressing it. The present position of these two countries did not determine the trade's international status. Public sentiment was that "this unnatural traffic ought to be suppressed." Public sentiment was "in advance of strict law." Even courts of justice — the British Admiralty courts were meant — had gone further in suppressing the international trade "than a more deliberate consideration of the subject would justify." Whatever might be "the answer of a moralist" — was there a slight bow to Story? — a jurist had to search for a "legal solution."

That the slave trade was contrary to the law of nature, the Chief Justice said, "will scarcely be denied." Every person had a natural right to the fruits of his own labor. That proposition was generally admitted. A necessary result of this admission "seemed to be" that no person had a right to deprive another of the fruits of his labor. War, however, had conferred rights in which "all have acquiesced." Victors, all agreed, were free to enslave the vanquished: "Slavery, then, has its origin in force." What was done "by general consent" could not be pronounced unlawful.

"Throughout Christendom," the Chief Justice wrote, "this harsh rule has been exploded." He stood on the brink of the proposition that slavery itself was now illegal. But Africa, he immediately added, was not within Christendom. Throughout Africa, it was the law of nations that prisoners became slaves. Whatever might be the answer of a moralist, it was not contrary to law for the colonial empires to continue their established practice of purchasing these prisoners. The international slave trade was legal under international law.

The Proof of Ownership

"The general question being disposed of," the Chief Justice wrote, "it remains to examine the circumstances of the particular case." General question — particular case; the antithesis was not unusual for Marshall, who inclined to decide the big abstract question one way and give the losers on the abstract issue a victory on the facts. Half of his opinion had been devoted to establishing the legality of the slave trade in international law. Would he devote the rest to showing that these slaves were free?

He encountered at once an intractable obstacle. Lacking an active seventh member, the Court could divide three to three. On the central contentions in the argument developed by Key and Wirt, the Court did divide three to three. Had the claimants the burden of proving that the Africans were slaves, not free men? Had the claimants sustained the burden when they had not identified the slaves individually? On these critical points Marshall was silent because the Court was split. The Chief Justice wrote: "Whether on this proof, Africans brought into the United States, under the circumstances of this case, ought to be restored or not is a question on which much difficulty has been felt." In this single sentence and by this passive voice, he compressed the debate within the Court and concealed who had felt "much difficulty." He would not, he wrote, state the reasons pro and con. As the Court was divided, "no principle is settled." No principle was settled, but the necessary result of the division was that the decree of the lower court awarding the Africans originally on the *Antelope* to the Vice Consul of Spain was affirmed.

This was not the end of the opinion. A separate question was whether the Spanish Vice Consul had the burden of proving the number of Africans who had been aboard the *Antelope*. This question could be answered without asking whether the Africans were free human beings or not: in any suit for property an owner had the obligation to show the extent of the property he claimed. The Court held that the Vice Consul of Spain had here a burden to sustain which he had not met.

Grondona and Ximenes had testified that there had been 166 Africans on board when the *Columbia* struck, Smith and Brunton that there were 93 or 90-plus. The libel had claimed only 100 from the *Antelope*. It was improbable, the Chief Justice remarked, that a large number of Africans could have been procured in the ten days between the time the first attacker had depleted the *Antelope* and the taking by the *Columbia*. Weighing this improbability and the inconsistency in the initial claim, the Court was "rather disposed" to believe Smith and Brunton. But even if the testimony was equally cogent on each side, the claimant failed — he had the burden. At most, 93 had been proved to be aboard. On this matter of fact, cast in the form of law by the invocation of burden of proof, the Court reversed Johnson and Cuyler and returned to the original position of Clerk Glen which put 93 as the Spanish maximum.

The Chief Justice took up separately the claim of the Vice Consul of the King of Portugal. For over five years, he observed, no Portuguese had appeared in court to claim the property the Vice Consul had libeled. No individual had been designated as the probable owner: "This inattention to a subject of so much real interest, this total disregard of a valuable property is so contrary to the common course of human action, as to justify serious suspicion that the real owner dares not avow himself."

Portuguese diplomats had been as cooperative with the plaintiffs in 1825 as in Abbé Correia's heydey. A letter, said the Chief Justice, had been supplied the Court from the Secretary of Foreign Affairs of Portugal with instructions on the means of transporting to Portugal the slaves claimed by the Vice Consul. The letter said nothing about particular Portuguese owners. It was not contended that the slaves belonged to the Portuguese Crown. The case had been argued on the basis that the slaves belonged to some individual. "Who is that individual?" the Chief Justice asked.

The doctrine enunciated by Justice Johnson in *The Bello Corunnes* that a vice consul was a proper party to sue for property was now subjected to a large exception. The Court, the Chief Justice said, would take notice of the notorious fact that under the flags of other nations the slave trade was carried on by Americans and others whose own country prohibited participation in the trade. Under these circumstances, the claim of Portuguese ownership by the accredited diplomatic representatives of Portugal would not be taken at face value by the Court. The long and unaccountable absence of any Portuguese claimant furnished "irresistible testimony that no such claimant exists." The Portuguese share was reduced from 130 to zero.

The Vote

That Story and Thompson had been outvoted 4 to 2 on the status of the slave trade is clear. That Story had prevailed on the question of the Portuguese owners, and that Johnson on this point had been outvoted 5 to 1 or 4 to 2, is also obvious. That 4 or 5 of the justices insisted against Johnson that the Spanish claimant must prove the extent of his original property is equally certain. But how did the 3 to 3 division, so significant in its consequences to the Africans, occur?

Story and Thompson must have voted to reverse Johnson's entire decree. If the Chief Justice had stayed with them, it is improbable that both Washington and Duvall would have deserted him, and the vote would have been 5 to 1 or 4 to 2 against Johnson. If the Chief Justice had in fact gone with Story and Thompson, it is unlikely that he would have passed in such complete silence over the crucial absence of identification of the Africans, and it is unlikely that the subsequent course of the case would have been what it was. Proof in a case for freedom, Marshall had written in *Mima Queen and Child,* was not different from "general cases in which a right to property may be asserted." The Chief Justice must have joined Johnson in holding that the property was sufficiently identified.

Circumstantial evidence suggests that Marshall was followed by Washington. After all, he had written that domestic slaves were "secured to us by sanctions equally valid with those by which we hold every other species of property." He would have seen that a different standard of proof where slaves' freedom was at stake would upset that uniformity of sanctions. He was the President of the Colonization Society, but not everyone in the Society had Key's devotion to the Africans' cause. When Marshall's opinion was published in the Society's journal *The African Repository,* it was given special prominence and described as "very able." The description corresponded to Washington's general estimate of his Chief. Accepting Marshall on the legality of the slave trade, he would not have quarreled with his treating the Africans as property when it came to proof. To make a counterblock of three against Marshall, Washington and Johnson, Gabriel Duvall must have acted on his lone dissent in *Mima Queen and Child* and insisted that the right to freedom was more important than the right to property and consequently, that evidence of enslavement must be more exacting than the proof of title to merchandise.

The Lottery

Did the Supreme Court of the United States, led and shaped by John Marshall, approve a lottery as a way of choosing the Africans who were free? Haste, lack of attention or conflict in the Court left the lottery in limbo.

The Chief Justice wrote, apropos of the Spanish share: "The individuals who compose this number must be designated to the satisfaction of the circuit court." The reference to "individuals" suggested that particular Africans had to be identified as having been on the *Antelope* at Cabinda. The Chief Justice, however, also referred to the Africans "which were brought in" and "which may be designated as Spanish property." The neuter pronoun seemed to refer to things which could be divided as things in bulk are divided. "Designated" was a term compatible with proof or lot or some third manner of selection. When the Chief Justice had said that no individual Portuguese owner had been "designated," he had not meant "proved" or "chosen by lot," but merely "pointed out." To designate the slaves would seem to mean merely to point them out; arguably, pointing excluded the use of chance.

The Supreme Court, like any appellate court, did not have before it the persons whose lives it was touching. It would be the task of an inferior tribunal to apply its rulings directly to the human beings affected. The Chief Justice's decree — the legal directive to the lower court attached to the opinion — reversed Justice Johnson and Judge Cuyler on the Portuguese claim, reduced the Spanish share from 166 to 93, and provided for deducting from the 93 the "ratable loss" which had occurred through death. This meant that there would have to be a recalculation of the number of Africans actually free. The Chief Justice's directive ended: "the said decree of the circuit court is, in all things not contrary to this decree, affirmed." Read literally, Marshall's decree approved the lottery. It was left to the lower court to decipher what he meant when that court came to decide which individuals were free and which were property.

· 7 ·

Sam, Lucy, Joe . . . and Boatswain

The Embarrassment of Counsel.
June — July 1825

The "law in Somerset's case," Governor George M. Troup of Georgia informed the Georgia Legislature on June 7, is "a favorite one with our learned Attorney General." William Wirt, "representing the United States," Governor Group declared, "had appeared before the Supreme Court and said in a ripe and splendid argument, that slavery, being inconsistent with the laws of God and nature, cannot exist. Do we want more . . . ? This is left to your decision." In this fashion the argument of William Wirt in *The Antelope* was used to fan secessionist sentiment already rising for other reasons in the State of Georgia.

Senator Berrien was partly responsible. He had grumbled to the Governor about the drift of Wirt's presentation. No doubt what he had put as the logic of Wirt's position had been taken by the Governor to be his actual argument. Berrien was embarrassed by the Governor's exaggeration, by the implication that he had silently condoned Wirt's outrage, and by the fact that he could not now pointedly support the Governor. He made it known that he had been absent on other business when Wirt had delivered his argument. He had not intended what he said to the

Governor in private to be the basis of an official communication to the Legislature.

The Attorney General was also embarrassed. In July 1825 he wrote each Justice of the Supreme Court asking if the Justice recalled him saying what Governor Troup said he had said, of saying that the Government of the United States should interfere at all with slavery in the several states. The replies he received showed him innocent of such radical ideas. Bushrod Washington declared that neither in express terms nor by inference had Wirt maintained such propositions. He added: ". . nor can I imagine in what way that could have been made to apply with the least propriety to the subjects under discussion."

Impasse. December 1825 — March 1826

Sitting as a court of two in Savannah at the beginning of December 1825, Justice Johnson and District Judge Cuyler split on the meaning of Chief Justice Marshall's decree. One said that the lottery had been approved. One said that it had been rejected. Who stood where is inferable. The lot had been Johnson's solution to an impasse in 1821. Overruled on two issues, obstinate, and after all privy to what his colleagues had said to each other in March, Johnson would not easily have admitted that the Supreme Court had disavowed his appeal to the Almighty. Charged with responsibility to carry out the Supreme Court's decision and unable to agree, the judges were unable to act.

At about the same, the President transmitted his First Annual Message to Congress. He made only a half-sentence allusion to the slave trade: "if some few citizens of our country have continued to set the laws of the Union, as well as those of nature and humanity, at defiance by persevering in that abominable traffic, it has been only by sheltering themselves under the banners of other nations, less earnest for the total elimination of the trade than ours." Adams at least acknowledged what Wirt had told him at the time of *La Jeune Eugénie* — the American slave trade depended on foreign flags. But he did not propose to do anything about it. He made no allusion to the Act in Addition, the outcome of *The Antelope* in the Supreme Court, or the state of the Africans in Savannah. He did transmit to Congress the Report of the Secretary of the Navy which stated that the Supreme Court's decision had placed "125 to 130" Africans "under the control of the government." Arrangements were being made to send them to "the agency for recaptured Africans." He was of course unaware that the judicial machinery had stalled in Savannah.

News of what had happened in the Circuit Court had still not reached Washington on December 28, 1825, when the Secretary of the Navy, Samuel L. Southard, wrote the Agent at Cape Mesurado, Liberia, that the Africans from Georgia would soon arrive: "It will be your duty to take immediate measures to prepare for their reception." Timber and tools had already been shipped. "The buildings must be finished in the simplest and cheapest manner."

News from Savannah had not reached Chief Justice Marshall on January 1, 1826, when he began the year with what looked like the execution of a New Year's resolution. He wrote to Secretary Southard to ask if the Navy had transported the Africans of the *Antelope* to Africa. Did something about the decision of the past year pinch Marshall's conscience? It cannot have been often that the Chief Justice inquired on his own initiative about the fate of litigants in his Court.

By January 5, 1826, the news had reached the Navy. Southard answered Marshall's inquiry by telling him that the Navy had been prepared, but the Circuit Court had divided. He added that in anticipation of sending them to Africa, many of the Africans "had been brought into Savannah by those to whom they were hired and put in the custody of the marshal."

Southard at the same time wrote Habersham that the result in Savannah had "created surprise, as it was supposed that the question had been clearly settled by the Supreme Court." Now "all that can be done is to expedite the settlement of the question, and the collection of the Negroes, as much as possible." Habersham was urged to give the case his "active attention" and report his "progress." The Administration appeared to believe that progress could be made in Savannah, where the Circuit Court had adjourned, and not in Washington, where an appeal lay. The "collection of the Negroes" — the turning them back to Marshal Morel — was to be expedited, even though no one now knew when they would be moved to Africa.

John Morel's appointment was due to expire on January 23. He owed his office to the patronage of William Crawford. Secretary of State Adams had written in his Diary that Morel's hands were ineffaceably stained with blood. President Monroe had removed the Africans from Morel's care. On December 13, 1825, President Adams sent Morel's nomination to the Senate for a term of four more years as Marshal. For the duration of the Africans' experience of the legal system, Marshal Morel resumed responsibility for them.

The quandary of the Circuit Court could only be resolved by a new decision in the Supreme Court. This time there was no argument and no opinion and no delay. On March 16, 1826, one year after its first decree, the Court issued a certificate acknowledging the controversy in the Circuit Court over "the mode of designating the said slaves to be delivered." The Supreme Court now decreed that the slaves "be designated by proof made to the satisfaction of that court." With the words "by proof," the Court appeared to have rejected the Rabelaisian method of decision by lot. The Court had, however, retained the word "designated." Only further argument would show whether its second decree was significantly less ambiguous than its first.

Designation. May — December 1826

In Milledgeville in May 1826, Richard Wylly Habersham once more presented the case to Justice Johnson and Judge Cuyler. By Marshall's decree, the Spanish share was a maximum of 93, with ratable loss still to be determined. The judges entered an order that the Spanish claimant "designate by proof the Africans, not exceeding 50."

How was the "50" reached? Marshall had provided that ratable loss should be calculated by the total number of deaths being divided by a fraction whose numerator was 93 and whose denominator was the total number of Africans taken by the *Columbia.* No testimony had ever established the denominator. The Circuit Court ignored this part of the Supreme Court's directive.

The Circuit Court reduced the Spanish share by 46 percent, a figure apparently reached by taking the number of Africans delivered in July 1820 to Marshal Morel, 258, and subtracting the number of Africans who had died in Savannah. From the percentage used, it may be inferred that 116 persons had died during the six years their case had been before the courts. Reduced by 46 percent, the Spanish share came to 50.

The order issued in Milledgeville in May could not be put in effect until the winter, when Johnson and Cuyler met in Savannah and the Africans collected by Morel were available for identification. From May till the end of November 1826 no judicial action occurred. An inquiry, however, came from the Adams Administration. Secretary Southard wrote Richard Wylly Habersham on August 10:

> It is extremely desirable that something be done towards removing the Africans of the General Ramirez out of the country, as the expense of their maintenance will soon absorb the amount appropriated by Congress.
>
> It is understood that the Supreme Court determined the mode in

which the division was to be made among the claimants, and it can only remain for the circuit court to give the necessary order.

Will you be pleased to inform me what has been done since the last term of the Supreme Court, and whether there is anything absolutely to prevent the delivery of the Africans? If only a part of them could be sent off, it would reduce the expense of their support. I also wish to ascertain what is their present situation, and if an arrangement cannot be made with the Portuguese claimant for the delivery of a portion, or the whole, without an order of court, should it be impracticable to obtain it immediately.

Southard's inquiry appeared to reflect the concerns of President Adams. He seemed unaware that the Supreme Court had decreed division by some manner of proof, so that the free Africans could not be known until the evidence was taken. The letter referred to the claimant as Portuguese — a slip, but it was at the time of the Portuguese complaint about the privateers of José Artigas that Adams had first heard of the case. The letter worried that the expense would absorb the appropriation. No money in fact had been spent since July 1822, and no money had to be spent unless the marshal kept the Africans at his expense. But the exhaustion of the appropriation had been Adams' worry since he had first been told of the Africans in 1820.

As the Circuit Court convened in Savannah for its winter session, 1826, Marshal Morel entered the case in person. He submitted his bill to the court. He asserted a lien on all the Africans of the *Antelope.* If his bill was accepted and not paid, he stood to become the owner of those who had been in his care.

Morel's bill covered the period till the end of the May term, 1823, the first three years of the Africans' stay in Savannah. For this period, his charge was $35,755. For the next period up to January 15, 1826, the Marshal said most of the Africans had been hired out, and his charge was only $519.91. For the last eleven months, he said, all had been hired out, and he made no charge. The Marshal acknowledged payment of $3,349.50 and asked for $32,945.41, to be satisfied by sale of the Africans. If they were taken at their appraised value of $300 apiece, 110 of them would liquidate his claim.

Johnson and Cuyler gave their decision at the beginning of December 1826. "The Court," said Justice Johnson, "cannot help feeling that the paying of bills of such an extraordinary amount as those of the Marshall in this case must expose this Court and the administration of justice in this Country to certain imputations." After six years of litigation, after two decrees by the Supreme Court, after six decisions participated in by Justice Johnson himself, the case was ending with the costs approximating the value of the property at issue: the Court and the administration of justice in the United States were exposed to imputations.

If Johnson had inquired of the Navy, he would have discovered that the Marshal had already been paid $20,206.98 by the Navy for the period up to July 1822. He might also have discovered that Habersham's investigation had led the President to refuse the Marshal's bill of $12,659 for 1822-23. If he had recalled testimony he himself had heard, he would have wanted an estimate of what the Marshal had made in hiring out Africans before 1823 or in using them on his own plantation. Justice Johnson concentrated on the rate at which Morel had calculated maintenance.

The rate had been set by Johnson himself in 1821. It was sixteen cents a day per African, "the very lowest charge we can find any precedent for," the rate at which county jails in Georgia provided for slaves charged with a crime, one-third that provided for the maintenance of prisoners of war. The rate, Johnson said, could not be regarded as extravagant. It was not his fault that the case had gone on so long. He had had to set some rate. "What could I do?" he asked. "The United States regards the subject of this suit as men and not things."

Johnson accepted the Marshal's bill. Who should pay it? In affirming the Circuit Court in 1825, the Supreme Court had said nothing about expenses. The judges now interpreted the Supreme Court's decree to mean that expenses should be paid only in proportion to the property acquired. The Portuguese Vice Consul, having gotten nothing, should pay nothing. The Spanish Vice-Consul should pay a proportion determined by the share he actually received. The difficulty was, who should pay the rest? With the Spanish share reduced, the rest was over $20,000.

One to one, Justice Johnson and Judge Cuyler split again. One judge thought that the Marshal had a lien on all the Africans. The United States would have to pay the unpaid balance before any could go free; alternatively, the Africans freed by the United States would have to be sold to satisfy the claim. One judge thought that Morel had no property in the Africans. He would have to turn over the portion of the United States without conditions and put his claim for expenses to the Treasury or Congress. Divided once more, the Circuit Court was unable to enter an order on how the lion's share of the Marshal's bill should be met.

Of less importance to the judges — at least it drew no opinion from them — was the designation by proof of the Africans who were Spanish property. On this subject, however, they did conduct a hearing. William Richardson testified that in 1820 he had been in charge of work on the fortifications of Savannah when Mayor Charlton had assigned him 50 Africans to use. He supervised their labor and fed and counted them three times a day. The Marshal and "a gentleman" had come out to inspect the Africans. The gentleman had clapped his hands. The Africans had "appeared generally to move towards him upon his giving the signal — many of them appeared to know the man very well." Had all the Africans on the fortifications recognized the gentleman's handclap? Habersham asked the question on cross-examination. Richardson said that he could not say that all had done so.

Marshal Morel testified that he had accompanied Domingo Grondona on a tour of the places where the Africans of the *Antelope* were kept; that Grondona had clapped his hands and called out a foreign word to the Negroes at work on the fortifications; that "the Negroes approached him generally and appeared to recognize him as a former acquaintance." He had taken Grondona to the house of Mr. Haupt. The three Africans there shook Grondona's hand and were "then recognized by Grondona." He had taken Grondona to Dr. Berthelot's, where Grondona recognized a boy named Tom. He had taken Grondona to his own plantation where over 100 of the Africans were kept. Grondona had pointed out a number as Africans he knew. Asked on cross-examination if all the Africans on his plantation had recognized Grondona, the Marshal said "No." He could not remember the number Grondona had identified as his former cargo.

Henry Haupt testified that he had had three Africans, Sam, Lucy and Joe, when "the Spanish gentleman" had visited his house. Joe was then ten years old. The Africans had "appeared to understand" the language Grondona spoke to them. On cross-examination, he said the Africans had not responded to other gentlemen in the same way. Dr. Berthelot testified that he had received two Africans from the Marshal, but did not remember any Spanish gentlemen coming to his house. Berthelot did recall Tom, who had once been in his possession and was now before the Court.

"The Negroes of the cargo of the *Ramirez* to the number of ——," so Clerk Glen recorded, with the unfilled blank a permanent memorial fo the informality of the occasion, were then ordered "to be collected" in front of the Court House. Richardson was instructed to "designate" those whom he remembered working under him on the fortifications. He pointed to 33: Jim,

Sam, Jack, Billy and McCase, all of whom still worked for him; Joe, John, Titus, Tom, Dick and Prince, now held by Mr. Adams; Jack, held by Michael Brown; Sandy, Jean-Pierre, Jack, Bob, George, Jim, Ned and another Jack, held by Ebenezer Jenckes, a toll road contractor; Dick, held by Dr. Barlow; McKinda, held by Judge Charlton; Simon, held by Isaac Conner; Tom, Sandy, Jim, Ned, Tom, John, Peter, Tony and Quacca, held by Thomas Young; and Boatswain, held by Adam Cope. He could remember two more, both named Jack, Richardson added; they were in the possession of Mr. Jenckes. This made the total he had designated 35.

Sam, Ned, Bill, Dick, Tony, two Johns and Boatswain were the names of winners of the lottery of July 18, 1821. Since some Africans had the same names, complete certainty is not possible, but it is not improbable that some or most of these eight men now identified by Richardson were ones who had been certified as free by the decree of Johnson and Cuyler confirming the lottery at the Christmas Term in 1821. One at least we are sure of — that African whose seamanship had won him the appellation "Boatswain" was a free man by federal decree in 1821 and a slave by federal decree in 1826.

No testimony was introduced to show that the persons designated by Richardson in December 1826 had been those who had stepped forward to greet Grondona in December 1820. Grondona himself was not present to undergo examination. Counsel suggested that he was dead. His testimony in 1821 that he had recognized 150 of the Africans from the *Antelope* was added to the record of the 1826 hearing, for completeness. No one commented that he had recognized 57 more Africans than the Supreme Court had ruled were ever on the Spanich *Antelope*.

Without discussion of the admissibility of the evidence, without analysis of its ambiguities, without explication of the standard of proof which they were employing, Justice Johnson and Judge Cuyler held that 39 Africans had been designated by proof to their satisfaction as Spanish property. All of those mentioned by Richardson, plus Sam, Lucy, Joe and Tom, were now decreed to be slaves. They were to be delivered to the Vice Consul of Spain on payment of his share of the Marshal's costs.

Designation by proof satisfactory to the Circuit Court had had one advantage over a lottery for the Spanish claimant. The men on the fortification had been, in Marshal Morel's words, "the primest of the gang." These now made up the bulk of the Vice Consul's share. In all, he had 36 men, one woman, and two boys.

The Third Appeal. January — March 1827

Richard Wylly Habersham appealed once more to the Supreme Court of the United States. He asked the Court to find the Spanish proof inadequate and all the Africans free. He asked the Court to dismiss the Marshal's lien that stood in the way of freedom even if the Spanish claim failed. He asked that the Vice Consul of Portugal, having brought a groundless case, pay his share of the Marshal's bill. He did not ask the Adams Administration if he should take the appeal.

The Attorney General was scheduled to act for the Africans and the United States on March 6, 1827. Argument in the Supreme Court would have begun about noon. A Cabinet meeting to consider the regulation of American commerce with British colonial ports was set for one o'clock. Wirt called the President early in the morning to ask to be excused from the Cabinet meeting. John Quincy Adams has recorded the reply he gave and the Attorney's General's response: "I told him I could not dispense with his attendance, and he came." The next week the Attorney General was firmer. Arguing a prosecution under the slave trade laws, he told the President that he "would be necessarily engaged in the Supreme Court" and refused to attend the Cabinet. When *The Antelope* was to be argued — did the President or he recollect the embarrassment caused by his argument in 1825? — Wirt simply noted, "I am *obliged* I find to be at the

President's at one o'clock. . . . The Court meantime has full employment from the *Antelope* which I have committed to Mr. Key."

Francis Scott Key opened and closed. Senator Berrien and District Attorney Ingersoll both appeared now in the name of the Vice Consul of Spain. The Portuguese Vice Consul, asserting only his nonliability for the bill, was represented by Richard Henry Wilde, a Georgia Congressman. No one argued for Morel. For the Africans, Key put the central issue to the Court, "there is no credible and competent evidence to identify them, or any of them."

The Antelope was no longer a big case in which the international status of the slave trade was at stake. The big case of the February Term 1827 was *Ogden v. Saunders,* on the power of the states to impair contracts by releasing debtors who had entered bankruptcy. Daniel Webster argued for the creditors, William Wirt for the debtors. Justice Johnson in his opinion said that the law should not be an instrument to bind a man to slavery if he had become incapable of carrying out a contract. Such an idea, he said, was worthy only of Africa. To use the law in this way, he said, was to justify the ancient maxim, "*Summum ius est summa iniuria*" — "Supreme law is supreme injustice."

The Supreme Court in 1827 was the same as it had been 1825 and 1826 save for the appointment of Robert Trimble in place of Thomas Todd, deceased, so that the Court had seven voting members. Trimble was a Virginian who had moved West. He had been District Attorney of Bourbon County, Kentucky, and since 1817 the federal District Judge in Eastern Kentucky. His brother David was a Congressman from Kentucky who in 1824 had first switched from Crawford to Clay, and then in the election in the House had led the majority of the delegation in voting for Adams. Opposed by Berrien, he was acceptable to Henry Clay, whose opinion here was decisive. Trimble had been forcefully recommended to Clay by Robert Wickliffe, his old law associate in business for James DeWolfe — otherwise, Wickliffe had said, the Administration would lose Kentucky in the next election. Adams' only appointment to the Supreme Court, Trimble was to give the Court's last word on *The Antelope.*

Of the seven justices, Trimble was the least familiar with the matter. It would not have been usual to have Johnson give the opinion on his own decision in the lower court. It would have been appropriate for Marshall to follow up his opinion of 1825. Washington, Story and Thompson all knew a good deal about the earlier facts and issues; Duvall had cast a decisive vote on the standard of proof. If Trimble was assigned the case, it was either because the issues were no longer perceived as important or because he was the only judge not involved in the tie vote of 1825. He gave the opinion of the Court, four days after the argument, on March 10, 1827. It was a little over five years since the case had been docketed for consideration by the Justices.

The first and larger part of Trimble's opinion was devoted to the question of costs. On the issue which had divided Johnson and Cuyler, he held that Marshal Morel had a right to be paid from the United States Treasury, but he had no lien on the Africans. "It would, indeed, be extraordinary," he declared, that "the marshal, who is the servant of the government, and holds possession of the Africans merely by its authority, could obstruct the operations of the government merely by a claim for compensation for his services."

Whether sixteen cents a day was the right rate, or an overcharge, Trimble said he would not say. The Spanish claimants could not complain. The right amount to be paid by the United States could be certified by the lower court in accordance with the statute on the compensation of federal marshals. The Court had no power to give a judgment against the United States for costs, but it was "not to be doubted" that the President would pay the Marshal out of the $100,000 appropriated in 1819 to suppress the slave trade. No doubt Key had never been briefed that the Navy had, after investigation, refused the Marshal's bill; and

Trimble, without information from counsel, blandly assumed that the Marshal's charges were proper.

The Vice Consul of Portugal, Trimble declared, should pay nothing. Implicit in the 1825 decree of the Supreme Court, he said, was the principle that costs be apportioned in the ratio of Africans received. The position of the Portuguese Vice Consul in the litigation had been "very peculiar." Under the circumstances in which these Africans were captured and brought into the United States, "it was his duty to interpose a claim for part of them on behalf of the subjects of His Majesty the King of Portugal." That claim had been sustained in the district and circuit courts. The "general propriety" of the claim had been "recognized by the former decree of this court."

"No such claimant exists," the Chief Justice had written in 1825. Justice Trimble did not refer to this language, nor did he refer to any language of the Supreme Court which recognized the general propriety of the Portuguese claim. He did not explain how it had been the Portuguese Vice Consul's duty to carry on a lawsuit on behalf of nonexistent subjects of the King of Portugal. He did not comment on the Chief Justice's view that the true claimants had been afraid to come forward in a court of the United States. He did not ask how the Vice Consul and his lawyers could have been unaware of the fraud.

After disposing of the financial issues, Justice Trimble said, "It only remains to be inquired, whether the Circuit Court erred in directing thirty nine of the Africans to be delivered to the Spanish claimants." Francis Scott Key had argued that "there is no credible and competent evidence to identify them, or any of them." "We," Trimble wrote, "are not of that opinion. We think, that under the peculiar and special circumstances of the case, the evidence of identity is competent, credible, and reasonably satisfactory, to identify the whole thirty nine."

Trimble summarized the testimony of Grondona in 1821 and the testimony of Richardson and Marshal Morel in 1826. He offered no comment on the biases, hiatuses, and improbabilities attending this evidence. He did not recall the Chief Justice's view of the unreliability of Grondona's word. He did show some awareness of how far the Court's credibility was being stretched: "We think" he said, "this evidence was sufficient, under the very peculiar circumstances of this case, reasonably to satisfy the mind of the identity of thirty nine of the Africans as belonging to the Spanish claimants."

The circumstances of *The Antelope* were "peculiar and special" in Justice Trimble's opinion. They became, like the position of the Vice Consul of Portugal, "very peculiar" after he had reviewed the evidence. Reasonable satisfaction seemed less than full satisfaction. The mind, nonetheless, said Robert Trimble, was sufficiently satisfied by the proof offered. The mind he referred to was the minds of at least a majority of the Justices of the Supreme Court.

· 8 ·

The Interest and Humanity of Congressman Wilde

Transportation. June — August 1827

On June 2, two and one half months after Justice Trimble's decision, almost seven years after the capture of the *Antelope,* Secretary Southard consulted the President on a problem he had encountered in getting the liberated Africans to Africa. The Navy had hired the *Norfolk,* a transport, to move them under the supervision of Dr. Peaco, the United States Agent in Liberia. Shortly after arriving in Savannah, Dr. Peaco had died. Southard was looking for a suitable replacement. Meanwhile, as the President observed, the *Norfolk* had overstayed the time contracted for in Savannah "and now remains at a charge of demurrage to the public."

President Adams had one suggestion: to appoint Dr. George P. Todson as Agent-in-Charge. Todson was a Louisianan who had served two years as an assistant surgeon in the Army when he was convicted of the embezzlement of government property, fined and dismissed from the service. The President had refused to set aside the court-martial or the punishment. Todson's lawyer in November 1826 had warned Adams that his client planned to assassinate him. The lawyer had "believed that it was no idle menace; that the man was desperate, and upon this subject, perfectly mad." The President had thought, "I am in the hands of a higher Power." He had met Todson, discussed his problems and remitted his fine. Later, on May 30, 1827, Todson had asked the President to help him get appointed a clerk in the War Department; his name was fresh in Adams' mind when Secretary Southard called. The President said that had he believed all his misfortunes "had originated in the badness of his temper, that would constitute the principal objection to his appointment." The President nonetheless proposed that he take charge of the Africans. The forgiven would-be assassin stood before him as a real object of benevolence.

Southard made inquiries about him and told the President on June 4 that he was doubtful about his appropriateness. Todson called on the President. He was "extremely anxious" about obtaining the appointment. The President again referred him to Southard, who, on June 12, appointed him Agent-in-Charge at an annual Salary of $1,600. His salary as an Army Assistant Surgeon had been $45 per month. Adams told Todson that he hoped his conduct would be such as to justify his selection.

The President in his Diary made no observations about the Africans in Savannah who were to be in the doctor's care. He did not connect them with the *Antelope,* the events which had come to his attention as Secretary of State in the summer of 1820, the spring of 1821 and the fall of 1822, or with the argument that had taken place on the eve of his Inauguration. He did not refer to them as liberated persons. In his Diary he spoke of the Africans of the *Antelope* as "a number of negroes adjudicated to the United States as having been illegally imported."

In Savannah John Morel, M.D.G., had one more task to perform in connection with the Africans adjudicated to the United States. In the spring and summer of 1827 he assembled them in Savannah and put them aboard the *Norfolk.* He charged for embarking 134 Africans; and he embarked 131.

How many of these persons assembled by the Marshal had been on board the *Antelope* when the *Dallas* had taken her off the coast of Florida the afternoon of June 29, 1820? Eleven or twelve of those who boarded now were under the age of ten. None of them, it may be guessed, had been infant slaves aboard the *Antelope*. They must have been born in Georgia, and they should be subtracted from the total of 131 to determine the number who had arrived in Savannah from Africa. Probably, then, as many as 120 of those embarked in Savannah had been among the 281 whom the *Dallas* rescued from the *Antelope*.

Dr. Todson took a month to arrange his affairs and complete the boarding process in Savannah. The *Norfolk* sailed with the Africans under his supervision on July 18, 1827, and reached Cape Mesurado forty-one days later. A child, an aged paralytic and another adult died en route. Two babies were born. Three women and one man among the arrivals were invalids. One man was dumb. One man was classed by Dr. Todson as an idiot. The other survivors had no noteworthy medical problems.

Liberation. August — December 1827

In May of 1825, two months after the Supreme Court's first decision in *The Antelope*, the managers of the Colonization Society had approved the Constitution of Liberia. Article I of the Constitution declared that "all persons" in the land should be "free and entitled to all such rights and privileges, as are enjoyed by the citizens of the United States." Article IX said, "This Constitution is not to interfere with the jurisdiction, rights and claims of the agents of the United States over the captured Africans and others, under their care and control, so long as they shall reside within the limits of the Settlement." The "captured Africans" were the Africans liberated from slave ships.

The agents of the United States to receive the Africans, authorized by the Act in Addition, had become a "United States Agency." Sometimes they described their post as "United States

Agency for Liberated Africans." Sometimes they gave its title as "United States Agency for Recaptured Africans." Whether the Africans were called captured, recaptured or liberated, the Constitution of Liberia recognized them as being in the care and control of the Agency.

At the urging of the Navy, the Agency had already built accommodations to receive the arrivals from Georgia. They consisted of two L-shaped buildings, one and one half stories high, 14 feet wide and 72 feet long. Each building contained a store room and "five spacious apartments." Each apartment contained a "loft for recaptured Africans." It was not the plan of the Agency to house all 130 arrivals in these quarters for a long time.

Nine days after the landing, Dr. Todson wrote Secretary Southard to describe "the terms on which the recaptured Africans will be placed in the families of colonists, and at service in Monroe and Caldwell":

> Laboring men, not mechanics, and wives — for the pair —
> 7 bars of goods of assorted merchandise, or \$3½ in merchantable country produce per month.
> To be given quarters, dry and capable of being kept perfectly clean; also a supply of decent clothing.
>
> Mechanics — same, except wages are to be \$8 per month.
>
> Laboring men — same, except wages are to be \$2½ per month.
>
> Laboring single women — same, except wages are to be \$1 per month.
>
> Laboring girls under 18 — no payment, and service till 18.
>
> Laboring boys not grown — no payment, and service for 3 years or until 21.

"No recaptured Africans," Todson added, "are to be sent into the country to sit down, for trade or other purposes, unless, or longer than, attended by their guardians; nor are they to be permitted to straggle off, and waste their time in idleness among the country people, without suitable means to recover them."

Jehudi Ashmun, the representative of the Colonization Society and the principal Agent of the United States in Liberia, also reported to Southard on the arrivals from Savannah and on a handful of Africans from New Orleans who had been shipped with them on the *Norfolk:* 60 men and 41 women were, by mid-September, at work in families; 10 men, 3 women, 2 children and the "idiot" were employed by the government at "liberal wages" $50 a year; 19 women and children were awaiting situations. All adults, Ashmun wrote, would receive lands and would have the privileges of colonial settlers if their conduct for twelve months "shall not prove them unworthy of the civil rights attaching to landed property in the colony."

One of the Africans, bathing in the Mesurado River, was eaten by a crocodile. A three-year-old child died after thirty hours of fever. As to the future of the remainder, Jehudi Ashmun wrote the Secretary of the Navy in December 1827:

> These people have proved, far beyond expectation, orderly, peaceable, and industrious. Only a solitary offence deserving corporeal punishment has come to my knowledge, and this grew out of a sudden exasperation of passion. Five marriages have been solemnized; and the irregular connexions of the unmarried strictly prohibited, and, as far as is known, prevented entirely. Seven women, having one or more small children each, not obtaining situations in the families of the settlers, have been employed in the best manner I could place them in the public service. Three of them wash and cook for the public laborers, the rest have situations in the *Colonial Infirmary and Orphan House,* where they enjoy the strictest paternal superintendence of the manager of that establishment, and are fully employed, without any actual increase of the sum total of the public expense. It has proved a truly auspicious circumstance, when only the temporal lot of these people, and their restoration to Africa, are considered, that more than 40 of their number have brought with them that best of all personal endowments, a simple and imperfect, but serious and practical knowledge of Christianity. The true religion operating on such minds, exists and displays itself only in its influence on the life and character. And this is only salutary. I trust their good conduct during their probationary year will secure them the good wishes and patronage of all in the colony whose friendship can

> hereafter be most useful to them. A part of them is destined at the end of the year to the newly projected settlement at Grand Bassa; another division I hope to provide for on the Stockton, midway between Caldwell and Monroe. The lands of both districts are good, and *equally* good. The third or remaining part of the company, consisting of single women and minors, will remain attached to the families of the settlers, and accede, in time, to the privileges of the American emigrants.

Midway between the settlements commemorating the fifth President of the United States and the second Clerk of the Supreme Court, on the river bearing the name of the captor of *La Jeune Eugénie,* the remnant from the *Antelope* were to be finally placed. The impact of American law upon them, which had first been felt that June morning off the coast of Florida when the *Dallas* had given chase to the *Antelope,* had substantially terminated.

Christmas in Savannah. December 1827

The three decrees of the Supreme Court had not determined any legal fees. These were settled for the proctors of the victorious Vice Consul of Spain by Judge Cuyler acting for the Circuit Court at the December Term in Savannah. *The Antelope* had been a battle of lawyers far more than a battle of clients. The lawyers for the Portuguese Vice Consul had acted for nonexistent Portuguese; the lawyers for the Spanish Vice Consul had acted for a dead man. Behind the shadowy formal parties had stood persons too distant or too fearful of the criminal law to exercise strong control over their advocates. On the side, the real parties at interest, the Africans, had had no say at all in telling their lawyers what to do. Now the lawyers for the private parties were to be compensated. Judge Berrien submitted a bill for $1250, Judge Charlton a bill for $800, and the executor of the estate of Charles Harris a bill for $500. Clerk Glen found that Judge Berrien had already received $150 from the sale of the *Antelope* in 1820; but he did not reduce his bill. Charlton and

Harris had received $600 apiece in payment for their services prior to the Supreme Court decision. The Clerk reported that Charlton and Harris were not entitled to more than an additional $250 apiece for their later services in the Circuit Court. They were now owed a total of $500.

Negotiation among the lawyers must have followed this report. By decree of Judge Cuyler, Senator Berrien was awarded $850 and Charlton and the estate of Harris were awarded $500 apiece. Charlton and Harris received $500 more than the Clerk had said they were entitled to, Judge Berrien $400 less than he had asked. It may be inferred, from circumstances yet to be set out, that Judge Berrien was entirely agreeable to this bargain.

Outstanding legal fees were, therefore, $1850. Salvage owing Captain Jackson was $1950 (39 Africans x $50). Court costs were $920.30, of which the Vice Consul of Spain had already paid all but $73.30. The Marshal's charges for maintenance were reduced from $18,476, as they had appeared in the Clerk's Report of 1826, to $6347. Judge Cuyler decreed that after paying Jackson, the Marshal, the court and the lawyers, the Vice Consul might take the Africans the court had had judged to be the property of Cuesta Manzanal and Brother. What he needed to obtain them, then, was $10,220.30.

The cash was found, and everyone was paid. Senator Berrien as proctor for Jackson received the $1950 in salvage and as counsel for the Vice Consul of Spain received the $850 remaining as his fee for his two appearances in the Supreme Court. Morel was paid. Harris' executor and Judge Charlton were paid. The court charges were paid. What had happened was that, before Judge Cuyler had entered his decree, a purchaser had been found who was willing and able to put up the money necessary to acquire title to the Spanish property.

Clerk Glen's valuation of the slaves in 1827 was $300 per African — the same as the valuation he had made in 1821, although the slaves were now domesticated and chosen from the primest, and the market price of slaves in general had risen. The Clerk protected himself by saying this appraisal was of Negroes "subject to the condition of exportation." The Court had ordered them to be removed from the country within six months, and the purchaser had to assume a bond of $400 per slave, which he would forfeit if the slaves were not exported in six months.

Thirty-nine slaves valued as the Clerk had valued them were worth $11,700. The purchaser put up $10,220.30 to meet the expenses fixed by the Judge. The difference of approximately $1500 may have been paid by the purchaser to the original owner; Senator Berrien told the Senate that it was. No receipt for this sum appears in the record, and for all that it discloses the Vice Consul of Spain, or Cuesta Manzanal and Brother, took nothing after seven years of litigation and vindication of their claim by the Supreme Court of the United States. The Spanish owner, as will shortly be seen, was in league with the nonexistent Portuguese owner. Together they received the sum of zero, or $1500 at most, for property once worth over $75,000 if all of it could have been secured. However cunning the friends of Abbé Correia had been, the chief financial beneficiaries of this lawsuit were not the litigants but the lawyers and Morel.

By the time the transaction was completed, the day after Christmas 1827, the Marshal had no more than 37 Africans to deliver. One had died during the session of the Court, and his death was noted in Cuyler's final decree. Another, Morel reported, died during December. A total of 37 were delivered as slaves to the new owner. That the purchase price was not reduced suggests that the new owner had a way of recouping the loss. He had paid a little over $10,000, or perhaps $11,500; but the true valuation of the slaves, without a bond for re-exportation, must have been closer to $15,000. This was the price Berrien was to tell the Senate, and $14,800 was the amount that the Clerk had set as the value when calculating the bond. If the slaves could be kept in the United States, the purchaser stood to make several thousand dollars on his investment.

The settlement at Savannah was not the last payment to Senator Berrien. As proctor for Jackson he had already filed a claim with the United States for the government bounty payable on free Africans. Shortly before the *Norfolk* had departed Savannah in July with the 120 survivors, he had received $3750 (150 Africans x $25). Four months after the cash distribution in December, he received another $1350 (54 Africans x $25). Jackson had much earlier been paid $400 on the 16 Africans judged free by Justice Johnson. The total bounty paid under the Act in Addition amounted to $5500.

The basis for the bounty is not difficult to perceive. Berrien took 258, the number of Africans delivered by Jackson to the Marshal in July 1820. He subtracted 38, the number found to be slaves in Morel's hands by Judge Cuyler on December 1, 1827. He inferred that 220 must represent the number who had been free when the *Antelope* had arrived in Savannah, and whether they were alive or dead now, he obtained, in installments, the bounty for all of them.

How the bounty was divided is not as easy to perceive. Only one payment, the first $400, was made to Jackson by name. The *Dallas* had been condemned as unseaworthy in 1824, and Jackson himself as a consequence discharged from the Treasury's employ. He would not have been in a position to finance seven years of litigation with a United States Senator acting as his advocate. It is not impossible that the rest of his share he had assigned as contingent compensation to Berrien. It is not unlikely that in any event Berrien had a right to a great portion of this sum. He had presented Jackson's case with overwhelming success in the trial court and with great success in the Circuit Court. When Judge Cuyler awarded counsel fees in Savannah, Berrien asked nothing from Jackson. It is improbable that he, who had shaped the case in Savannah and in Washington, should have gone without payment from his first client. The easiest way of assuring his compensation would have been an assignment of the later bounty; that it finally came to $5100 was his windfall.

One lawyer who had been part of the case from the beginning was absent when the cash was distributed in Savannah. Richard Wylly Habersham had resigned as United States District Attorney in 1826, the month following the Supreme Court's third decision in *The Antelope.* Henry Clay as Secretary of State accepted his resignation on behalf of the President without comment on his services. At the same time Clay wrote Justice Johnson that the President wished him to designate Habersham's successor. The Justice was told to add the name of any "competent member of the bar" to a commission which was sent to him in blank. "You no doubt," wrote Secretary Clay, "possess ample information on that subject." The new District Attorney, Matthew Hall McAllister, was actually nominated by Adams only on December 19, 1827, and his nomination was before the Senate as it came to consider a remarkable petition affecting the fate of the Africans in Savannah.

Sunbeams from Cucumbers. December 1827

The distributor of the cash to counsel in Savannah, the purchaser of the enslaved Africans of the *Antelope,* was Richard Henry Wilde, a lawyer from Augusta, Georgia, and a newly elected Congressman. He had first appeared in the case in Savannah in 1826, representing the Vice Consul of Portugal in his protest against bearing any part of the Marshal's expenses, and had then argued the Portuguese case in the Supreme Court. But his very first connection with the case had been in June 1825, when Berrien had sought his help in extricating himself from the difficulties caused by Governor Troup's reaction to his argument in *The Antelope.* Anglo-Irish, of the same family that produced Oscar Wilde, he had come to America as a boy, taught himself law, and became Attorney General of Georgia in 1811 at the age of 22; he had in fact been a junior ally of Berrien since 1817. When he won Vice Consul Sorrell's exoneration from paying the Marshal's bill, Berrien wrote congratulating him on "Sorrell's deliverance . . . You will have a better opinion of Courts of Admiralty, since you find they can do justice in the event, altho' like 'the extraction of sunbeams from cucumbers,' the process is difficult." In the first part of 1827, Wilde was a frequent visitor at Berrien's home in Georgetown.

On May 22, 1827, Wilde set out to Berrien the basic plan that was to govern the disposition of the 30-odd Africans whose enslavement had been affirmed by the Supreme Court. He began by disclosing an arrangement that might have been guessed to exist between the Spanish and the anonymous Portuguese claimants, but would not be known without his letter. It is one more circumstance suggesting that the Spanish were no more Spaniards than the Portuguese were Portuguese:

> While I was in Savannah Mr. Sorrel absolutely declined prosecuting his claim to half the 39 negroes of the Ramirez, but insisted on assigning it to me. I could not well refuse to receive the ajst [adjustment] after urging him to assert his rights, but I attached little importance to it at the moment, because I understood the Spaniards could not or would not take the negroes, upon the terms required of them, in which event they would go to the U.S. & be free, a result which I would not only, not oppose but rejoice at. I learn however that as the Marshall would have no lien for his bill in that event, arrangements are made or making by him that they *shall* be bonded and sent out of the country, by some arrangement with the Spaniards which will secure him in whole or in part his balance of cash about I think $7500. Now if these people could be free by any act of mine, they should never hear of the Portuguese claim so far as I could control it. If they are to be slaves, I am disposed to give them the chance of taking up their abode as slaves in the U.S. provided the Govt will assent, & the risk & expense on my part is not too great. I shall at all events buy about 20 slaves shortly — now if I can get these poor devils in consequence of this arrangement somewhat lower than

> I should buy others & they will be better off with me, than they would be in Cuba, I do not see, why I should by any sickly fastidiousness neglect at once interest & humanity . . .

The Spanish and Portuguese, as a species of insurance, it appeared, had agreed in advance to split fifty-fifty any slaves awarded by the court. Sorrell, the Portuguese Vice Consul, believed that his share, subject to the payment of expenses and the condition of exportation, was not worth very much, and had assigned it to Wilde for his legal services. Morel, afraid that both claimants of the property would abandon it rather than pay his charges, $18,476, against their share, had reduced his bill and appeared willing to make a deal. Armed with these facts, Wilde saw an opportunity to make a profit without risk if he were not deterred by "any sickly fastidiousness." He put forward this proposal to Berrien:

> My plan is simply this. If the Portuguese title thus made is good, & the Spaniards will acknowledge or be bound by a division of the slaves according to it — which you must judge of and arrange for me — I then propose to buy off the Marshalls claim, on the one half — which I suppose might be done for $2 or $3000. If they can be taken into possession immediately I propose to leave them with you until next winter when their fate would be decided — provided always they would be of use to you in your growing crop & not an expense. My plan then is this. I will apply to the Govt of the U.S. to do one of two things: either re-imburse me the actual expenses paid by me & take the Africans, or pass a law cancelling the bonds for exporting them, if given, or dispensing with such bond if not given — in other words allowing them to remain as slaves. If they adopt the first alternative, I am only just where I was, at liberty with my money to buy negroes which I do not want at all events until next winter. If the second I have the slaves I want for my Florida project with this advantage. Instead of taking unwilling or depraved beings to whom that destination would appear a banishment, I get a set of good slaves to whom such a fate will be comparatively a benefit. Furthermore to preserve consistency throughout it will be necessary to select such as either have no ties here, or whose wives are in the hands of gentlemen & men of humanity who will either buy the husband or sell the

> wife on fair terms. In this way I propose to collect a group who will be perfectly willing to remove, & happier in their removal than they could be in the destiny otherwise awaiting them. I persuade myself this is not a visionary project either in point of interest or humanity. But there are many difficulties in it in which I require your professional, aye & your friendly advice & assistance. . .

The "Florida project" he spelled out further: "The delegate from Florida" — Joseph White, the territory's representative in Congress — "offers me very advantageous terms in a joint sugar plantation, which will be under the management of his brother . . ." The latter, "a practical industrious farmer and honest man" would have the active responsibility, so "we shall be at liberty to neglect the plantation ourselves as much as we shall certainly do." Wilde was, in fact, to retire to Florence and study Dante on his profits.

Throughout this revelatory letter, Wilde maintained his self-image — benevolent, liberty-loving, gracious. Perhaps the only man in the world who could have been the friend of both Henry Clay and Charles Sumner, Wilde was celebrated for his charm and for his love of the humanities. His greatest claim to fame was his authorship of "The Summer Rose," a poem said to have been favorably noticed by Byron. It was not for one humanist writing another to let his motives be reduced to the sordid calculations for profit of a slave dealer. He closed: "My feelings toward those poor creatures induces me to wish them free. But if slavery is their destiny I desire to render it as endurable as slavery can be . . . I shall have a set of workers who will be too happy in escaping an evil so dreadful to their imaginations, that Florida will be to them indeed 'a land of flowers' . . ." As he noted, they would be "good slaves," broken by seven years in Georgia to life on a plantation.

His reliance on his friend was complete, because Berrien would handle Congress, although Wilde could not imagine that Congress would be reluctant to grant the favor he would need.

Berrien might, if he chose, "take the Spanish moiety & join them to the Florida colony, as a partner yourself." Upon all these subjects, Wilde told him, "I give you carte blanche"—appropriately modest words for the junior plotter entering a case which from the beginning had borne Berrien's imprint.

As the plan outlined in May took shape under Senator Berrien's direction in November, its contours and emphasis, but not its object, changed. When the court decree, already described, was being prepared in Savannah, the mechanics of the plan were settled. By petition dated November 30, 1827, Wilde informed Congress that he was acting at the request of the Africans themselves. As counsel in the case he had learned "of the repugnance of these people to depart from a country to the language and habits of which they were accustomed; where easy labor was imposed, and kind treatment received." He had been "struck with the cruelty of separating them from their wives and children, to send them into slavery in a Spanish country." If it meant "some risk and trouble to himself," Wilde meant "to afford them the chance of becoming free, or at least of suffering servitude only in that mitigated form, already familiar to them, in a state of society to which they had become reconciled, and in the bosom of their families." He asked Congress to cancel the court-required bond given as security that he export the slaves.

Action in Savannah and Washington was synchronized at a speed which did not even give time for correcting discrepancies in the record. Judge Cuyler's decree fixing the expenses and actually setting the bond was entered on December 1, the day after the petition was framed. By December 12, Wilde had offered the Africans to the Colonization Society at cost and had received an answer. The Board of Managers thanked him for his "humane proceedings" and declared it was "not compatible with the principles of the Society, or within its ability to reimburse him." The Managers (Key still their moving spirit) expressed the hope that Congress would act in their stead, make the payment, and permit the Society to transport the ransomed Africans to Liberia. The Managers were induced to say further that if Congress would not buy the Africans at least it should "absolve Mr. Wilde from the obligation of tearing these unfortunate persons from their families and sending them into slavery beyond the limits of the United States." In this hasty response of the Managers, it is possible to suppose the one effect on Key's actions of his cousinly connection to Charlton. If Cousin Tom had vouched for Wilde and indicated that fair compensation for his own legal services were at stake, the swift cooperation of the Managers would be comprehensible.

In Savannah itself the solidarity of the bar was never more evident than in the expeditious working out of the arrangements. That the earlier payments to Charlton and Harris on behalf of the Vice Consul of Spain had been made was attested to by Francis Sorrell, Vice Consul of Portugal. Payment to Berrien on behalf of "Cuesta Manzanal and Brothers" (sic) was made by attorney William Gaston. Gaston then became one of three citizens of Savannah joining Wilde's petition to Congress and attesting that the facts appended to it were correct. Gaston was joined in this role by one Joseph Cummings and by William Law, the old lawyer of the acquitted pirate, John Smith, and more recently Senator Berrien's associate in legal work for the state of Georgia. The Executor of Charles Harris who had to negotiate the share owed the estate of the senior partner of Harris and Charlton was John Morel, the busy Marshal of the United States.

No later than five days after the Colonization Society's resolution, sixteen days after the decree and ten days before Morel delivered the Africans to Wilde, the petition of Wilde to cancel the bond was introduced to the United States Senate by Senator Berrien, now the third ranking member of the Judiciary Committee. The day it was introduced, Wilde's petition was referred to this committee headed by Martin Van Buren. Three days later, December 20, a bill granting the petition was reported out and received its first reading. On its second reading, on December 31, when an explanation was asked, Senator Berrien gave a capsule history of the case of *The Antelope.* Congressman Wilde, he observed, had put out a total of "about $15,000," an "aggregate amount being greater than the value of the slaves."

To arrive at this aggregate, Berrien put the salvage paid by Wilde as $4500 (the decree said $1950) and the Proctors' fees he had paid as between $2000 and $3000 (the decree said $1850). He added that Wilde had paid $6000 to the Marshal and $1500 to the owner. He did not attempt to explain the discrepancies between his figures and those in the decree attached to the petition signed by Wilde, nor did he call attention to them. He said nothing of Wilde's plan to move the Africans to new land in Florida. He ended his explanation to the Senate by stating that Wilde had bought the Africans "from motives of humanity alone."

American Enslavement. January — May 1828

Passed by the Senate, the bill canceling the bond came before the House of Representatives on January 7, 1828. Philip Pendleton Barbour of Gordonsville, Virginia — the former speaker of the House, the present Chairman of the Judiciary Committee of the House, the future Justice of the Supreme Court — presented the case for the bill's enactment without further consideration by a committee. During the seven years the matter had been in the courts, Barbour said, "these unfortunate creatures had been detained in the custody of the Marshal, and in this interval, many of them had married, and become heads of families, had been partially domesticated with us, and were desirous of remaining in this country." Mr. Wilde had acted to assist them "in the pure kindness of his heart."

A private bill, whose enactment would be a courtesy to a colleague, might have been expected to pass without discussion and without dissenting votes. John W. Taylor of Saratoga, New York, "one of the severest and keenest debaters that ever sat in the House," and John C. Wright of Steubenville, Ohio, a supporter of the Adams Administration, objected to a vote without a report. Barbour disclaimed any desire of precipitancy, and the bill was tabled. Three days later Barbour took up the bill again, and Taylor again asked for a report on the facts. "The question might be," he said, "one which involved the liberty of 37 human beings." With great penetration he added, "Even the slave trade itself has, by some persons, been attempted to be justified on the ground of humanity."

Henry W. Dwight of Stockbridge, Massachusetts, declared that he was personally acquainted with Richard Henry Wilde and had the highest respect for him. Wilde had told him how due to a failure in the decree of the court to specify who was free and who a slave, the case had gone on eight years. "The humanity, however, of the southern gentlemen had not left them all this while imprisoned. They had been put out on healthy plantations, where many of them had acquired the relations of husband and wife, parent and child, and had formed attachments to the country." Congressman Wilde had been employed as counsel in the case and become acquainted with these slaves. When it was known they would be sent away, "they came to him as to their only friend, and, implored, with tears, that they might not be sent away."

Charles F. Mercer of Aldie, Virginia, the usual spokesman of the Colonization Society in the House, said the Society had been unable to buy the Africans from Wilde because it had 1800 persons wanting passage to Africa. He suggested that the House find out how much Wilde had actually spent. The United States could then reimburse him and return the Africans to "their native land." Debate continued on this ground — Wilde's friends seeking only cancellation of the bond, his opponents seeking to purchase and liberate the slaves.

Charles A. Wickliffe of Bardstorm, Kentucky, and George R. Gilmer of Lexington, Goergia, spoke for the bill. John Wright, the Congressman from Steubenville, then gave the history of the *Antelope* in the courts, bringing for the first time to the congressional debate a substantially accurate account of the case's course. He continued to press for a full committee report. Peleg Sprague of Hallowell, Maine, spoke in favor of the government "reimbursing Wilde and putting the Africans at liberty in Africa. Charles Miner of Westchester, Pennsylvania, moved that the Committee on the Judiciary explicitly consider this possibility. The Committee should be instructed to inquire "whether it would not comport with the interests of humanity, the principles of justice, and the honor of the Government to adopt efficient measures to restore the Africans to the country and home from which they have been cruelly and illegally separated."

Gilmer of Georgia asked "how this House was going to alter a solemn decision of the Supreme Court of the United States." There were "no persons in the world who held the slave trade in deeper detestation" than the people of Georgia, but he could not vote to take Congressman Wilde's property from him. Wilde had paid $15,000 to the "Spanish claimant," and he had not offered to sell this valuable property to the United States.

John Randolph of Charlotte, Virginia, objected that Miner's motion referred to Africans "illegally separated" from their own country. There was no evidence that they had been unlawfully acquired. "They were as lawfully taken, probably," he said, "as any slaves who were brought into South Carolina and Georgia since the adoption of the Constitution, under the clause in the Constitution which permitted the traffic in slaves for a limited time." The decision of the Supreme Court was itself "positive evidence that these persons were not illegally taken."

Once again the notion was invoked that positive law in the narrowest sense was decisive. Like Berrien and like Marshall, Randolph concluded, "I am now bottoming myself upon law —

upon sheer law." Miner answered, "I did not intend to speak in the precise terms of the lawyer." Legality "should be determined by the higher laws of God and humanity. Those were the laws to which I referred." But he withdrew his motion.

Friday and the weekend intervened and on Monday, January 14, the Committee on the Judiciary reported out the bill canceling the bond. The pace suddenly slowed. No action was taken until April 26, when Barbour asked the House to consider it as a Committee of the Whole.

Taylor of New York moved that the United States pay Wilde $11,700, the appraised value of the slaves subject to exportation, on condition that he deliver the Africans to the Colonization Society for transportation to Liberia. The motion was defeated 39 to 99.

David Woodcock of Ithaca, New York, observed that Wilde's asserted motive was to keep the Africans from being slaves in Cuba, but in forbidding slaves to be taught to read, in allowing forcible separation from wives and children and in refusing their emancipation on the payment of their value, the laws of slavery in Georgia were more severe and offensive than the laws of Cuba. He did not understand how cancelling the bond was "required by motives of humanity." On April 28, Aaron Ward of Mount Pleasant, New York, again moved that the United States reimburse Wilde on condition that he surrender the Africans to the Colonization Society. His motion added that the Africans should be given the choice of going to Liberia or staying, in freedom, in the United States. The motion lost without a roll call. The bill to cancel the bond was put to the House and carried 92 to 82.

At the beginning of May 1828, President John Quincy Adams signed the bill and made it the law of the United States. Its enactment effectively ended the last chance for freedom afforded the 37 enslaved Africans of the *Antelope* by the American process of law.

Albemarle, James Monroe's home where in August 1820 he had decided the policy his Administration had pursued for four years in respect to the Africans of the *Antelope,* had a last coincidental connection with them. In the spring of 1828, for over $5000, Monroe delivered the slaves of Albemarle to be transported for use or sale in Florida. In this fashion he carried out in person one-half of the Jeffersonian program of emancipation and deportation of Virginian Negroes. The purchaser of Monroe's slaves was Wilde's partner, Joseph White, whose estate "Casa Bianca" was located not far from Monticello, Florida. By the fall of 1828 the remnant of the *Antelope,* except for a few sold by Wilde in Georgia to pay expenses, were at work on White and Wilde's development in Florida.

· 9 ·

Retrospect

Berrien's love for his family was, according to his modern biographer, "his most attractive characteristic." There are other public figures who acted in *The Antelope* who are more highly commended for their excellence as public servants. William Wirt, according to *Success in Life – The Lawyer,* published in 1850, had a governmental career as Chancellor of Virginia and Attorney General to Monroe and Adams which provided "the most exciting and encouraging example to the youthful aspirant to legal distinction." He was, in Secretary Southard's words, "the very *beau ideal* of a great constitutional lawyer." President Monroe is remembered for issuing the Monroe Doctrine and for keeping the country together during the stresses of the controversy over the admission of Missouri. His reign has been conventionally labeled "The Era of Good Feeling." In the minds of many it was the Silver Age of the American Republic. John Quincy Adams was not, as he wished he might be, an angel on earth. He was "the Department's greatest Secretary." He strove, in general, to exhibit "our great superiority to Europe"; in his own words that superiority lay "in political science, government, and political morality."

"Judicial objectivity," a modern historian writes, "was the approach evolved by the Marshall Court in slavery cases . . ." In *The Antelope,* adds another author, the Supreme Court "had little alternative;" it was bound to do as it did "by the legal system." In the words of Charles Warren, the biographer of the Supreme Court, the judges had to leave "the moral issue" to the legislature. William Johnson, according to his modern biographer, "consistently strove for a humane treatment of slaves; but he gave the law its way where the law was to him clear." Of Robert Trimble, Story said after his death that "no man could bestow more thought, more caution, more candor, or more research upon any legal investigations than he did," and the modern editors of *The Justices of the Supreme Court* have selected his opinion in *The Antelope* to accompany this eulogy.

Marshall himself has been placed in a niche almost beyond criticism. "When I consider his might, his justice, and his wisdom," Holmes has written, "I do fully believe that if American law were to be represented by a single figure, sceptic and worshipper alike would agree without dispute that the figure could be but one alone, and that one John Marshall." For all those Americans who in a secular age seek the equivalent of sacred authority, the utterances of the highest authority in the land have a pontifical function, and the Marshall Court, the creator of judicial supremacy in the American system, is specially hallowed. If, in the interstices of process in *The Antelope,* inertia, insensitivity, incompetence and even injustice are apparent, there must be rationalization congruent with the dignity of the Court. An anthropological perspective may provide such a defense.

The decent men who acted in this case were facing a situation unprecedented in their experience — the arrival on these shores of a substantial body of Blacks who by federal statute were as free as any white European. The decent men confronted this unprecedented situation in the context of a great political experiment less than fifty years old, at a time when the most informed of men feared for its continuance and when the most divisive of issues in the new Republic were those involving slaves. They acted in a society in which slavery itself had been accepted for almost two hundred years, so that it was second nature to think of Blacks as property in any legal context. They acted with an awareness that in any society where conflicts exist — that is, in any society outside of Utopia — perfect justice is impossible, compromises are inevitable and partial victories are the lot of humanity.

Each man acted as a role-player in a system, so that the conduct of each should be measured and understood in terms of his fidelity to his role. If the system is one of conflicting interests — and what system is not? — each one does his best if he represents well the interests confided to him. To play that role, he cannot dissipate his energies in altering the assumptions on which the system operates. Moreover, to repeat Aristotle's observation, man is by nature more a conjugal than a political animal. He has himself to feed, his wife to clothe, his children to educate. He has little time to look at the long-range consequences of his actions and no time to do someone else's job. If he acts at all as an official of the government, he must collaborate with others, delegate responsibility to others, depend on the fidelity and discretion of others. That network of cooperation is impossible to maintain if each oversteps his role.

If each one does the work assigned to him, much will be achieved. The world will never be Utopia with all wrongs righted. All kidnapped Africans will not be returned to Africa. But in *The Antelope* a substantial number of helpless aliens and their children were restored from slavery, and the Executive Branch personnel, the Congressmen and the Judges turned the wheels of government to accomplish this solid humanitarian end.

So might a nonjudgmental anthropologist trying to understand man as he is in his society, and finding the norms of conduct in the conduct he sees, judge the conduct of Adams,

Monroe and Marshall and the others who acted here. In a government whose power was precarious and restricted, he must conclude, no President could have done more for Negroes held in slave-holding territory than Monroe. In a nation exposed to foreign threats, no Secretary of State could have behaved differently than Adams in his prudent concern for plundered European property. In a society based on slavery, no lawyer could have been fairer in asserting the interests of his clients than Berrien. In any regime it is imperative that no official overstep his role, and no judge could have been more faithful to his role than Marshall. In a legal system based on a Constitution, statutes, and precedents, within the limitations set by American society in 1820, the decision in *The Antelope* was inevitable.

Even acts of cruelty like Morel's, of superstition like Johnson's, of venality like Wilde's, may be stripped of their moral hue and accommodated to anthropological explanation. Could more have been expected of a minor governmental functionary, unused to treating Blacks as persons, than Morel did? Was not Johnson's decree of a lottery understandable as the only solution of an intractable problem for a conscientious, puzzled and pious man? Did not Wilde combine profit-making with sentiment in a fashion that permitted him to enrich himself while harming no one? The dispassionate observer will see that Morel, Johnson and Wilde are, like Monroe, Adams and Marshall, merely products of their society or system.

The process was characterized by fraud — fraud on the courts by the lawyers pretending there was a Portuguese owner, fraud on the Executive by Morel and Berrien double-charging, fraud on Congress by Wilde and Berrien presenting themselves as philanthropists. Worse than fraud, there was a sustained assault on individual human beings. The process for a period of eight years enslaved all of the Africans and permanently enslaved 37 of them. In the process more of the free Africans perished than survived. A Dantean moralist would judge those who managed the process differently from the accommodating anthropologist. As God is just, he would ask, can the lawyers who enslaved or permitted the enslavement of these hapless humans in order to gain their fees escape condemnation as slavers? Can the politicians who procrastinated while these innocent victims were worked to death avoid damnation as moral imbeciles? Can the judges and legislators who turned their eyes from the reality beneath the legal process be stamped other than as hypocrites? If human beings entrusted to your care perish through your gross neglect, are you not guilty of manslaughter?

Against the rhetorical questions of such a moralist, the defenders of such famous men as Adams, Marshall and Monroe would be quick to protest. *The Antelope* occupied a tiny fragment of the careers of those who acted here; in public lives stretching over decades, it took up, at the most, a week of thought for any one of them. Shall such statesmen be condemned because they never focused on the facts of the case? Shall the work of a lifetime be overshadowed by an incident? Shall the reputation of the heroes of the Silver Age of the American Republic be blackened by a forgotten episode? Such are the natural retorts of the admirers of Adams and Marshall and Monroe. It is unfair, they say, to drag *The Antelope* into the lives of their heroes.

Hero worshippers and Dantean moralists are mirror images of each other, and they are equally mistaken. Both assume that history can judge a human being and, judging him, assign him to heaven or to hell. But a history, a circumlocution for historians, cannot judge whole human beings at all. Historians cannot penetrate the inner psyche where conscience acts. They cannot even know all the external circumstances affecting action. Although they must try, they cannot wholly step within another's skin and wear his soul. Nor can they judge without asserting the existence of ideals that are anachronistic projections of the sensibilities of their own day.

Yet there is another way of judging that does not require

omniscience and another way of measuring other than by anachronism. We may look at the acts done and measure them by the images or models accepted by Americans of the 1820's standards for action. That there were images, models, ideals in the minds of many Americans in 1820 is evident from the process of *The Antelope* itself. These operative paradigms were textbook ideals of what a court is, what a legislature is, what a President is. The case would not have happened except in a system structured by such ideals. The system is inexplicable unless some of those acting in it believed that a court is an impartial judge determining the rights of persons on the basis of evidence; that a legislature is a body of representatives making general rules for the public good; that the Chief Executive is obligated to carry out the laws. Even as these democratic paradigms of government were violated, they were acknowledged and the process channeled by them.

There is one paradigm which is fundamental to the understanding of these simple models of government. It is the paradigm of the person — that is, of the human being as an individual entity with rights and duties, with an origin and destiny that are like our own. Whether owed to revelation or won from human experience, that ultimate paradigm informed this process.

The notion of the person accounts for the original congressional legislation, it does not depend upon it. It is the basis of Habersham's claim in 1820 for the freedom of every African — "persons of color from some Eastern Kingdom of Africa." It forms the capstone of the arguments made by Francis Scott Key to the Supreme Court in 1825 and 1827 — a lottery cannot determine personal liberty; individuals cannot be disposed of in bulk. Against all the seductions of his environment, Habersham maintained his devotion to the individuals who were free. Gratuitously, passionately, charitably, Key worked for the salvation of the persons whose cause he championed.

Only one participant in the actions of the 1820's looked at

them in retrospect in terms of persons. In 1841, when Van Buren was President, John Quincy Adams defended Cinque and the other Africans who had risen in revolt on a Spanish slaver, *The Amistad,* and killed their captors. Old, out of power, rejuvenated, he read the decision in *The Antelope* and found it the greatest obstacle to the cause he now embraced. Before the Supreme Court iseelf he attacked what had happened. "[N]early three hundred Africans," he wrote, "had been kept prisoners of the United States." "Why," he asked, "were they not instantly liberated and sent home to Africa by the Act of March 3, 1819?"

Adams did not advert to his own role or that of Wirt, Monroe, Johnson, Trimble or Marshall, but he declared of the decision that it had been marked by "heartless sophistry." The process, he proclaimed, had manifested only "cold-blooded apathy to human suffering." Where had been the souls of those who had determined the outcome of the case? Their spirits had been "wedged in thrilling regions of thick-ribbed ice."

He put to the court a final rhetorical question, applicable to *The Antelope* as to *The Amistad,* and to himself as to Van Buren: "Is it possible that the President of the United States should be ignorant that the right of personal liberty is individual?"

Those who think in terms of power, of abstract national interests, of human beings in bulk, will always have a major role in governments. Those who suppose that the legal system is a self-subsistent set of rules existing outside of its participants and constraining lawyers and judges to act against their consciences will always be prevalent among lawyers, judges and legal historians. Those who think that every human action can be explained by the necessities of the prevailing social environment, the requirements of role-playing, the demands of national security will always be common among anthropologists, political scientists and sociologists. But every so often in a human heart the ice will crack, and a human person will acknowledge his responsibility for other human persons he has touched.

Abbreviations and Sources

All references to the United States District Court for the District of Georgia, here abbreviated to Dist. Ct., and to the Sixth Circuit Court, here abbreviated Cir. Ct., are, unless otherwise indicated, to documents now obtainable in the microfilm series of the National Archives, Records of the United States Supreme Court. Documents before December 1821 may be found in the records under *The Antelope,* 10 Wheaton. Documents from 1822 to 1827 may be found under *The Antelope,* 12 Wheaton.

The edition of John Quincy Adams' Diary by Charles Francis Adams, *Memoirs of John Quincy Adams* (1865), is referred to as Adams. The edition of James Monroe's papers edited by Stanislaus Murray Hamilton, *Writings* (1899), is referred to as Monroe.

Gerald Gunther very generously put at my disposal the notes he had made in preparation for writing a history of the Marshall Court. To these notes I owe President Monroe's letters to General Mason and Spencer Roane; Attorney General Wirt's three letters to his wife, his letter to Johnson and his letter to Swanson; Senator Berrien's two letters to Charles Harris, his letter to Governor Troup and his letter to Justice Washington; Justice Washington's letter to Wirt; Justice Story's letter to Justice Washington; Elizabeth Walker's letter to Justice Story; Charles Harris' letters to General Mitchell; Secretary Crawford's letter to Langford Cheves; Thomas U.P. Charlton's letter to Agent Williamson; and the letter of Congressman Wilde to Senator Berrien in 1827.

Notes

The notes are intended for the specialist reader, and the author has chosen not to have them keyed to the text by number.

Notes to pages 1-3

1. The Very Sensitive Agent

The Department of State. October 1818

At two in the afternoon: Adams IV, 134, October 17, 1818.

"a man of extensive and general literature . . . so much of a philosopher . . . as a familiar acquaintance . . . insinuating and fascinating . . ." Adams IV, 326, April 8, 1819. The spelling used in the *Grand Enciclopedeia Portuguese y Brasiliera* VII, 760, is adopted in preference to "Correa" as he appears in Adams, or "Corrêa" as he appears in Joseph E. Agan, *The Diplomatic Relations of the United States and Brazil* (1926), and Agan, "Corrêa da Serra," *Pennsylvania Magazine of History and Biography* (1925) XLIX, 1. On his botanical enterprise, see John W. Harsberger, *The Botanists of Philadelphia and Their Work* (1899), p. 8.

"the Presidential Trinity": Adams IV, 12, October 3, 1817.

Revision of the Neutrality Act: "An Act more effectually to preserve the neutral relations of the United States," 14th Congress, 2nd Session, March 3, 1817, *U.S. Statutes at Large* III, 270-371.

"not only the very sensitive and useful agent . . ." Monroe to Adams, August 3, 1820, Monroe VI, 149.

Correia's visit to Adams about the ship in the Patuxent: Adams IV, 134, October 17, 1818.

On José Artigas, the founder of Uruguay, see Edgardo Ubaldo Genta, *Historia de Artigas* (Montevideo, 1956); Eduardo Acervo, *José Artigas* (Montevideo, 1950); Juan Zorrilla de San Martín, *La Epopequa de Artigas: Historia de los tiempos heroicas de la Republica Oriental del Uruguay* (Barcelona, 1917); On the Portuguese taking of Montevideo, see Mariano Berro, *Anales de la Republica Oriental del Uruguay* (1895) II, 8.

The White House, Washington. November 1818

Conversation at Cabinet meeting of November 7, 1818: Adams IV, 164, November 7, 1818;

Instructions to Baltimore: William Wirt to Elias Glenn, November 6, 1818, *Official Opinions of the Attorneys General,* ed. Benjamin F. Hall, I, 249-252.

"questions of law . . . on the ground . . ." Wirt to Samuel Ingham, September 14, 1821, *ibid.,* I, 492-493. Italics in original.

"very unwilling to create a precedent . . ." Wirt to Secretary Crawford, April 11, 1823, *ibid.,* I, 613.

The Court House, Baltimore. November 1818

"[I] am directed by the President . . ." Adams to Correia, November 14, 1819, printed in *House Executive Documents* No. 53 (1852), 169; "prevailed upon the President": Adams IV, 319, March 28, 1819.

$1500 charge: Adams IV, 319, March 29, 1819.

"I have been engaged by the Portuguese Consul . . ." Wirt to Mrs. Wirt, November 19, 1818, Maryland Historical Society MS.

Correia's initial impecuniousness: *Grande Enciclopedeia Portuguese y Brasiliera* VII, 760.

The Department of State. March 1819

"any person" committing robbery: Act of April 30, 1790, First Congress, Second Session, *United States Statutes at Large* I, 113-114. Marshall's interpretation: *United States v. Palmer* 3 Wheaton 610 at 633-634 (1818), "a sample of judicial logic . . ." Adams IV, 363, May 11, 1819.

Artigas as Tecumseh: Adams IV, 308, March 19, 1819.

"feeble, inefficient men . . . employed by all the pirates . . ." Adams IV, 310, March 29, 1819.

"an exceedingly energetic . . ." *ibid.;* "as rotten . . ." *ibid.;* "I must take the brunt . . ." *ibid.*

"more atrocious . . . a great number of the vessels": Adams III, 454, December 23, 1816.

"under sanctified visors . . ." Adams III, 557, June 6, 1817.

"a barefaced and impudent . . ." *ibid.*

"American capital," covered by Spanish and Portuguese flags, with 50,000 Africans taken annually: "Queries proposed by Viscount Castelreagh to, and answers of, the African Society in London, December 1816," Annex B to the Protocol of the Conference of European Nations at Aix-la-Chapelle, February 4, 1818, printed in *House Reports* No. 92, 17th Congress, 1st Session, February 9, 1821, pp. 32-34. On the great importance of the slave trade to the Portuguese empire in Africa and Brazil, see Leslie Bethel, *The Abolition of the Brazilian Slave Trade* (1970) pp. 4-6.

The Department of State. August 1819

Confrontation with Bland: Adams IV, August 18, 1819.

"Sands' deposition is false . . ." Adams IV, 415, August 21, 1819.

"suborned witnesses . . . he acted by other persons . . ." Adams IV, 426-427, October 29, 1819.

The Port of Havana. August 1819

The *Antelope's* date of departure, "Certificate of the Captain of the Port of Havana": Dist. Ct.

The *Antelope's* origin, dimensions, tonnage, structure, ownership, and registration: *Ship Registers and Enrollments of Newport, Rhode Island (1790-1939),* Works Progress Administration, *Survey of Federal Archives,* 1941, I, 38. (There is a discrepancy of about ten tons from the tonnage ascribed to the *Antelope* in the Spanish papers.)

"Certificate of Property" of the Spanish Department of Marine: Dist. Ct.

"License to Trade for New Negroes," August 18, 1819: Dist. Ct.

Crew and arms of the *Antelope:* "Certificate of the Captain of the Port of Havana": Dist. Ct. Salary of American naval captain: *Register of Officers . . . on the 30th of September 1819,* p. 101.

"to take care of the sick . . ." Agreement, August 19, 1819: Dist. Ct.

2. The Suspended Tortoise

The Act in Addition. March 1819

Meeting of Mason, Jones, Key and Adams: Adams IV, 292, March 12, 1819. On Mason: Adams IV, 14, October 29, 1827.

"the pious informer, Frank Key": Adams VIII, 313, February 9, 1831.

"a Cypher": Key to Thomas U.P. Charlton (1824), Maryland Historical Society MS, printed in Edward J. Delaplaine, *Francis Scott Key* (1937), p. 235.

Officers of the Colonization Society: American Society for Colonizing the Free People of Colour, *Second Annual Report* (1819).

"nourished by the resources . . ." *ibid.,* pp. 10-11.

"had no design . . . free people of colour as may choose . . ." *ibid.,* p. 9.

"Fig leaves . . ." John Quincy Adams, *Argument in the Amistad* (reprinted New York, 1969), p. 39.

A crime to transport Africans or equip slavers: "An Act to prohibit the importation of Slaves into any port or place within the jurisdiction of the United States," March 2, 1807, 9th Cong., 2nd Sess., *Public Statutes at Large II,* 426-430.

"Should they have been turned loose . . .?" Wirt to the President, January 20, 1821, *Opinions of the Attorneys General* I, 451.

"the iniquity": Gales and Seaton, *The Debates and Proceedings in the Congress of the United States,* 15th Cong., 2nd Sess., XXXIII, 442, January 4, 1819 (debate on motion preliminary to the presentation of the slave trade bill). Congressman Charles Mercer explains and defends bill: *ibid.,* XXXIV, 1430, March 1, 1819. Passage of the Act, March 2, 1819: *ibid.,* 1433 (House); XXXIII, 280 (Senate).

The Act in Addition: *United States Statutes at Large* III, 532-534. For background of the Act, see Special Committee of the House of Representatives, Report, April 18, 1818, reprinted in American Society for Colonizing . . ., *Second Annual Report,* pp. 81-82; William E.B. Du Bois, *The Suppression of the African Slave Trade to the United States of America, 1638-1870* (1898), pp. 106-121; and P.J. Staudenraus, *The African Colonization Movement, 1816-1865* (1961), pp. 24-56.

"a ray of light . . ." American Society for Colonizing, *Second Annual Report.*

The Society's argument for a colony: Adams IV, 298-299, March 12, 1819.

"impossible that Congress . . . exceedingly humane weak-minded . . . so far as it is sincere . . . with all possible civility . . . To derive powers . . ." Adams IV, 292, March 12, 1819. On Chief Justice Symmes: Beverly W. Bond, Jr., "Symmes, John Cleves," *Dictionary of American Biography,* ed. Dumas Malone, 1943, XVIII, 258-259; on Symmes' polar proposal, see the petition presented on it to the Senate, March 7, 1822, 17th Congress, 1st Session, in Gales and Seaton, I, 278.

The First Test. April 1819

The President's instructions on the 30 or 40 Africans: Adams IV, 321-322, April 2, 1819.

Conference of Adams, Wirt and Crawford: *ibid.*

"in the abstract . . ." Adams V, 10-11, March 3, 1820.

"Oh, if but one man . . ." Adams IV, 524-575.

Adams solicited for money: Adams IV, 353-356, April 30, 1819. "traps for popularity": Adams IV, 299, March 16, 1819.

The Colonization Society's failure to buy the Africans: American Society for Colonizing, *Fifth Annual Report* (1822), pp. 103-110.

The President Persuaded. October—December 1819

"Mr. Crawford's fears . . ." Key to William Meade (1819), John Johns, *A Memoir of the Life of Right Reverend William Meade* (1867), p. 124.

"emancipation and deportation"; Thomas Jefferson, *Autobiography,* in *Works,* ed. Paul Leicester Ford, I, 78-79.

"I have always been friendly . . ." Monroe to Mason, August 31, 1829, New York Public Library MS, Monroe Collection, quoted with the permission of the Library.

"bring him back . . . My idea . . ." Johns, *Memoir of Meade,* pp. 124-125.

Key's lobbying to persuade the Attorney General: Key to Meade, in Johns, *Memoir of Meade,* p. 125.

"Appropriate any part . . ." Wirt to Monroe, October 14, 1819, *Opinions of the Attorneys General* I, 315-316.

"very probably, the correct one . . ." Wirt to Benjamin Homans, Chief Clerk of the Navy, October 16, 1819, *ibid.,* I, 317-320.

"the Act itself . . . without much consideration . . ." Adams IV, 436, November 10, 1819.

"I objected . . ." Adams IV, 476, December 10, 1819.

"shelter and food . . ." Monroe, *Special Message to Congress,* December 17, 1819, *Addresses and Messages of the Presidents of the United States,* ed. Edwin Williams (1846), p. 481

"obvious . . ." *ibid.*

A Privateer Launched. December 1819—January 1820

Departure date of the *Columbia:* John Morrison and Thomas Bradshaw, sailors of the *Columbia,* in Testimony, Dist. Ct., January 19 and February 15, 1821.

Description of the *Columbia:* Thomas D. Nicholson, carpenter of the *Columbia,* Examination before the Mayor of Savannah, July 11, 1820, *The Republican,* July 13, 1820; her 18-pound cannon, William Brunton, sailor of the *Columbia,* Testimony, Dist. Ct., January 18, 1821.

Two men aboard *Columbia* before recruitment of new crew; prize-sharing; and oaths of noncitizenship: Morrison, Testimony, Dist. Ct., January 19, 1821; commissions in blank: Adams IV, 301, March 16, 1819. See also Agustin Beraza, *Los Corsarios de Artigas* (Montevideo, 1950).

English-speaking crew: James Knight, second officer of the *Dallas,* Testimony, Dist. Ct., January 18, 1821; one Englishman: William Brunton; one Welshman: John Morrison; one Greek: John Stephen, Testimony, Dist. Ct.

Removal of Americans: William Brunton, Testimony, Dist. Ct.; cutter escort: John Smith, "Offer of Proof," Dist. Ct., February 13, 1821.

The *Columbia's* voyage: Nicholson, Examination, July 11, 1870, *The Republican,* July 13, 1820. In subsequent reports of the case she is referred to as the *Arraganta,* but to avoid confusion she remains in this narrative as the *Columbia.*

Cabinda. March 1820

"all he could carry off . . . the best slaves . . . a few left . . ." Vicente de Slavio, captain of the *Antelope,* "Declaration," March 30, 1820, notarized at Cabinda, filed in Dist. Ct.

The attack by the *Columbia: idem.;* 120 attackers: Grondona, "Declaration," August 5, 1820, Havana, filed in Dist. Ct.

Wreck of the *Columbia* and death or capture of Metcalf; course of the *Antelope;* incidents at Surinam and St. Bartholomew's; arming; and arrival off Florida: Nicholson, Examination, *The Republican,* July 13, 1820.

3. Safekeeping and Support by President Monroe

First Decisions. June — July 1820

The capture of the *Antelope:* James Knight, Testimony, Dist. Ct., January 18, 1821. Smith ordered the guns to be run out: Nicholson, Examination, July 11, 1820; *The Republican,* July 13, 1820. Smith's ship was out of food and water: John Jackson, Testimony, Dist. Ct., January 17, 1821.

Number of Africans: Knight, Testimony, January 18, 1821;

"the sickly months . . . almost certain death . . ." "An Act to prevent the introduction of passengers, who are aliens, into the port of Savannah, during the months of July, August, September and October," *A Compilation of the Laws of the State of Georgia,* Lucius Q.C. Lamar, compiler (1821), pp. 44-46.

"to save many valuable lives": Mayor Charlton, Proclamation, June 29, 1820; *The Republican,* June 29, 1820.

Habersham's order to Jackson: Monroe to Adams, August 3, 1820, Monroe VI, 145. On Habersham's lack of direction: An ambiguity existed in the Act in Addition. Was or was not the President free to deliver rescued Africans directly to his agents in Africa? The Act said "the vessel and her cargo" should be brought "for adjudication" into a port of the state to which the vessel belonged. If the Africans were cargo, they were subject to adjudication, too. The Act, however, used the phrase "negroes, mulattoes or persons of color" in distinction to the phrase "goods and effects." The Act provided a bounty of twenty-five dollars payable to the rescuers on "each person delivered." The Act said that the negroes, mulattoes or persons of color might be delivered to the United States marshal of the district into which they were brought or to the President's agents in Africa. All of this language suggested that persons of color were not cargo and that the President had discretion in determining their immediate destination.

The ambiguity was not resolved by the Judiciary Act of September 24, 1789, which governed the federal courts. The United States District Court had jurisdiction in "all civil causes of admiralty and maritime jurisdiction, including all seizures under laws of import, navigation or trade." It was not clear that the Judiciary Act qualified the Act in Addition. It was not clear that Africans rescued in the enforcement of a criminal statute could be the matter of a civil cause in admiralty.

The ambiguity, in the absence of decision by a court, could only be resolved by the Administration. The President in his Special Message in 1819 on the Act in Addition spoke of American ships taking Africans directly to Africa. He also spoke of Africans being delivered to United States Marshals. The President in a letter of July 24, 1820, to Adams on Africans who had been taken to the Canary Islands, said that he had supposed that the Canary Islands were not a place of deposit authorized by the Act, but that a capturing ship would "either bring the people of color to the United States or land them in Africa" (Monroe, VI, 143). The President implied that geographical convenience was the governing consideration. He did not advert to the fact that if Africans were landed in Africa, it would be substantially impossible for anyone to recover them as property. The President made no observations on the effect of the choice upon the Africans. The President gave no orders to resolve the ambiguity.

If the Africans were to be treated as cargo, the Act gave an option as to the port where their status should be adjudicated. The option existed if the captured slaver did not come from any particular state of the United States. Registered in Cadiz, the *Antelope* could have been brought into any American port. No orders had been issued by the President or the Secretary of the Navy or the Secretary of the Treasury as to ports which ships capturing slavers carrying Africans should avoid.

Claim filed July 15: *The Republican,* July 29, 1820.

Date of Habersham's letter: Adams to Habersham, August 10, 1820, U.S. Department of State, *Domestic Letters* XIX.

"calls for an early answer . . . disposition to be made . . ." Adams to Monroe, July 28, 1820, *Writings of John Quincy Adams,* ed. Worthington Chauncey Ford (1917) VII, 57.

Number of Africans reported: Monroe to Adams, August 3, 1820, Monroe VI, 145.

"without taking into account . . . will scarcely square the accounts . . ." Adams to Monroe, August 5, 1820, James Monroe, Papers, Library of Congress MS.

The President's Decision. July — August 1820

"that our Eastern bretheren . . . seduction of our citizens . . ." Crawford to Monroe, June 13, 1820, New York Public Library MS, Monroe Correspondence, quoted with permission of the Library.

"by the proper courts . . ." Correia to Adams, July 16, 1820, printed in an appendix to *A Report of the Secretary of State in response to the resolution of the Senate on April 13, 1820,* transmitted to Congress by the President, May 10, 1824; Gales and Seaton, 18th Congress, 1st Session, XLII, 3042. For a list of over 60 Portuguese ships said to have been taken by ships commissioned by Artigas, see Beraza, *Los Corsarios,* table at end of book. That a list of ships with Portuguese names and ports revealed nothing about the ships' ownership or business is suggested by looking at the ships with Portuguese, Spanish or French names and ports of origin listed as known or suspected slavers by the African Institution in 1825; see the list reproduced in *House of Representatives, 21st Congress, 1st Session* III, 348, p. 276. For a totally sympathetic account of Correia's diplomacy, see Agan, *The Diplomatic Relations of the United States and Brazil* (1926), pp. 82-114.

"with the best knowledge to be obtained . . ." Monroe to Adams, July 24, 1820, Monroe VI, 142.

Correia's announced purpose: "Mr. Correia is here, on his farewell visit to us," Jefferson to William Short, August 4, 1820, Jefferson,

Writings, ed. Albert Ellery Bergh (Washington, 1907), XV, 262. Correia's actual departure, Correia to Adams, November 23, 1819, *House of Representatives, Executive Documents* No. 53, p. 175. Astonishment that Correia still around: Jefferson to Correia, October 29, 1820, Thomas Jefferson, *Papers* (Library of Congress MS).

"rejoice to see the fleets of Brazil . . ." Jefferson to Short, August 4, 1820, *Writings* XV, p. 263; "piracies of Baltimore," *ibid.,* XI, 262. "it was out of the question . . . exceedingly irritable . . ." Adams, paraphrasing Jefferson's account to President Monroe, Adams V, 176-177, September 19, 1820.

Correia's visit: Monroe to Adams, August 3, 1820, Monroe VI, 149. On August 2 Monroe was at Oak Hill: Monroe to Jefferson, August 2, 1820, Monroe VI, 144.

The Savannah public ball, the arch of laurel, and the *Dallas:* Charles C. Jones, *A History of Savannah, Georgia* (1890), pp. 337-338.

"I return you Mr. Habersham's letter . . ." Monroe to Adams, August 3, 1820, Monroe VI, 145-146.

Foreign slave trade punishable by death: An Act to continue in force, "An Act to protect the commerce of the United States and punish the crime of piracy," and also to make further provisions for punishing the crime of piracy, May 15, 1820, 16th Congress, 1st Session, *United States Statutes at Large* III, 600-601.

Crossing out of "Instruct the District Attorney . . ." Monroe Papers (Library of Congress MS). In the printed text the omission is indicated by parentheses, Monroe VI, 145-146.

Date Monroe's orders reached Adams: *Department of State, Register of Letters Received* (National Archives), August 7, 1820. Adams to Wirt, August 10, 1820: *Attorney General's Records, Letters Received, State Dept., 1813-1849.* Wirt asked Adams for British Parliamentary Papers: *ibid.,* August 12, 1820.

Adams to Habersham, August 10, 1820: *Department of State, Domestic Letters* (National Archives) XIX, 108.

The District Attorney's Decision. July — August 1820

$75,000 — $100,000: the judicial appraisal was $300 per person; the Marshal used $400 when setting a reward for an African's return; and in 1828 the court used $400 when setting a bond. The annual maintenance of a Negro in custody was 16 cents per day: William Johnson, Opinion, December 1826, Cir. Ct., Value of prime slaves in Georgia, Ulrich B. Phillips, *American Negro Slavery* (1929), pp. 370-371.

Size of Savannah bar: an inference based on an estimate for 1830 in Jones, *History of Savannah,* p. 429.

Berrien's ancestry: Royce Coggins McCrary, Jr., *John Macpherson Berrien of Georgia (1781 — 1856): A Political Biography* (doctoral dissertation, University of Georgia, 1971; microfilmed, University Microfilms, Ann Arbor, Michigan, 1971), pp. 1-6; career at the College of New Jersey (Princeton), p. 13; early career, pp. 21-28; partnership with Davies and practice, pp. 35-42; position of Superior Court as supreme, p. 48; salary, p. 60; children, pp. 62-65.

"left an example . . ." Jones, *History of Savannah,* p. 420; "the American Cicero"; Lucius Lamar Knight, *Reminiscences of Famous Georgians,* II, 94.

Libel of John Jackson, August 25, 1820, Dist. Ct.; date of first filing for Jackson given in Habersham's libel as July 15, 1820, republished in *The Republican;* July 29, 1820.

Harris' public career: William J. Northern, *Men of Mark in Georgia* (1910), p. 32; *The Republican,* September 25, 1821; Morel as his executor, see Morel's Receipt, noted below in Chapter 8 under *Christmas in Savannah, December 1827.*

Charlton's public career: Jones, *History of Savannah,* p. 434; Northern, *Men of Mark,* p. 298. "the convenience of others"; Charlton to Williamson, July 21, 1818, University of Georgia MS (Telamon Cuyler Collection), quoted with permission of the University of Georgia. Examination of crew by Charlton, *The Republican,* July 13, 1820. Charles Mulvey: Obituary, *The Republican,* March 18, 1823.

Francis Sorrell: Notice of Marriage, *The Republican,* October 19, 1822; partnership with Douglas: *ibid.,* December 7, 1820. "150 or more . . ." Libel of the Vice Consul of the King of Spain, August 3, 1820, reproduced in *The Republican,* August 15, 1820. "130 . . ." Libel of the Vice Consul of the King of Portugal, August 3, 1820, *ibid.*

James Morrison: *The Republican,* September 5 and September 12, 1820. John C. Nicoll: Jones, *History of Savannah,* p. 549.

"very dear friend": Berrien to Harris, March 4, 1825, New York Public Library, Misc. MS, quoted with permission of the Library. Harris as Acting District Attorney: Harris to Mitchell, September 4, 1825, University of Georgia MS, Keith Read Collection, quoted with permission of the University of Georgia.

Habersham's birth and education, *Biographical Dictionary of the American Congress, 1774-1949* (Washington, 1949); presidency of the Union Society, Jones, *History of Savannah,* p. 549; St. Patrick's Day oration,

The Republican, March 17, 1825; contributions to the Colonization Society, American Society for Colonizing . . ., *Third Annual Report* (1820), p. 138; family background, Northern, *Men of Mark* I, 129, 140-141; his nomination, *Senate Executive Journal,* pp. 3, 184, January 3, 1820; his appointment and salary as District Attorney, *Register of Officers . . . on the 30th of September 1819,* p. 221*

Habersham's libel of July 15: reproduced in *The Republican,* July 29, 1820.

"persons of color . . ." Libel of the United States, August 15, 1820, Dist. Ct.

The Marshal's Decisions. July — October 1820

Auction by Morel: *The Republican,* July 29, 1820.

Original number of Africans and deaths accounted for: James Knight and John Jackson, Testimony, Dist. Ct., January 17 and 18, 1820.

"about 270 . . . 258 . . . presumed . . ." Adams to Habersham, August 10, 1820, Department of State, *Domestic Letters* XIX, 108.

"the African encampment" and disappearance of an African: Notice of Reward, August 8, 1820, reprinted in *The Republican,* November 11, 1820.

Payment to Morel by the Navy: Navy Department, "A Detailed Statement of the Sum Appropriated by the Seventh Section of the Act, passed the Third of March, 1819, in addition to the Acts Prohibiting the Slave Trade," *Senate Document* No. 3, 20th Congress, 1st Session (1827), p. 7.

Judge Davies' order denying release on bond: Dist. Ct.; "the primest of the gang . . ." John Morel, Testimony, Cir. Ct., May 9, 1826.

"pestilence confined principally to strangers . . ." *The Republican,* August 15, 8120; Board of Health report, *ibid.,* September 2. Aldermanic election, *ibid.,* September 5; mayoralty election, *ibid.,* September 12. "I feel it my duty . . . to remove beyond the limits of the city's atmosphere", *ibid.,* September 14; "cast despair around the city . . ." *ibid.,* September 21. Notice of Mayor Charlton's Proclamation: *Niles Weekly Register* XIX, 30, September 30, 1820. "very prudently and properly": *The Republican,* October 7, 1820; "the few inhabitants"; *ibid.,* October 10. "Savannah, the fever rages . . ." *Niles Weekly Register* XIX, October 21, 1820; deaths in epidemic, *ibid.,* XIX, 368, January 27, 1821; remaining population, *ibid.,* XIX, 176, November 11, 1820).

The Laughter of James Monroe.
September 1820 — January 1821

"very judicious and proper": Adams to Monroe, September 15, 1820, in Adams, *Letterbook, 28 September 1817 — 19 May 1831, "Public,"* Massachusetts Historical Society MS.

Adams on *Niles Weekly Register:* Adams V, 167, July 24, 1820.

"with the highest satisfaction . . ." Adams to Morel, November 15, 1820, Department of State, *Domestic Letters* XVIII.

"It is very desirable to save further expenses . . ." Thompson to Morel, January 13, 1821, printed in "Report of the Committee to which was referred so much of the President's message as relates to the Slave Trade," *House of Representatives Report* No. 92, 17th Congress, 1st Session, (1821), p. 92.

"Sir: The Act of the 3rd March . . ." Wirt to the President, January 27, 1821, *Opinions of the Attorneys General* V, 728-729.

"In execution of the law . . ." Monroe, Fourth Annual Message, November 14, 1820, *Addresses and Messages of the Presidents* I, 425.

The President "laughed heartily . . ." Adams V, 201, November 12, 1820.

4. Justice Bridlegoose

Trial One. December 1820

"alleged to be the property . . ." Indictment of John Smith, quoted in "Law Case — Piracy," *Niles Weekly Register* XIX, 318, January 13, 1821.

William Law's career: Jones, *History of Savannah,* p. 434.

"capitan de papel": *Niles Weekly Register* XIX, 216, December 2, 1820.

Law's argument for Smith, Davies' charge to the jury, Smith's acquittal: *ibid.,* 318, January 13, 1821.

Artigas' overthrow and exile: Eduardo Azevedo, *Anales Históricos del Uruguay* (1933) I, 259.

Trial Two. January — February 1821

Order to show slaves, November 17, 1820: Dist. Ct.

Grondona's origin: Certificate of the Captain of the Port of Havana, August 14, 1820, filed in Dist. Ct. Death of the *Antelope's* captain: Grondona, Deposition, June 21, 1820, San Juan, Puerto Rico, filed in Dist. Ct.

Testimony in Dist. Ct.: Jackson, January 17; Knight and Brunton, January 18; Grondona and Ximenes, February 13; Bradshaw, February 15; Smith, February 19. Grondona's depositions: August 5, 1820, Havana, and December 29, 1820, Savannah, both filed in Dist. Ct.

"a mere nominal claimant . . . the Negroes are the actual party . . ." Habersham, "Heads of the Argument in Behalf of the United States," appended to Habersham to Adams, March 12, 1821, Department of State, *Miscellany Letters.*

"from the moment he took those negroes . . . was used to cover . . . There is no evidence . . ." *idem.*

Opinion and Judgment. February — March 1821

Davies' biography: "Obituary," *The Republican,* May 5, 1829; presidency of Union Society, Jones, *History of Savannah,* p. 549; partnership with Berrien, *ibid.,* p. 428; appointment as federal judge and salary, *Register of Officers . . . on September 30, 1819,* p. 221*, and "biographical Notes of the Federal Judges," *Federal Cases* XXX, 1369. Crawford on Davies' character: Crawford to Langford Cheves, March 12, 1821, South Carolina Historical Society MS, quoted with permission of the Historical Society.

Berrien's resignation: *The Daily Georgian,* February 20, 1821.

Ruling on Smith with citation of *The Alerta:* Opinion of William Davies, Dist. Ct., February 21, 1821.

"However inhuman . . . However obnoxious . . . the circumstances in which . . . unreasonable and unjust . . ." *idem.*

Africans in Morel's custody, February 22, 1821,and calculation of Africans from the *Antelope* and division of shares, appraisal and salvage: George Glen, Report, Dist. Ct., February 27, 1821.

Confirmation of Report: Order of Judge Davies, Dist. Ct., March 6, 1821.

Date of Davies' resignation: Adams to Davies, May 2, 1821, accepting the resignation dated March 9, 1821, *Department of State, Domestic Letters.* "reunited their professional interests . . ." Notice, dated March 13, 1821, *The Daily Georgian,* May 11, 1821; "the claims of a numerous family . . ." obituary, *The Republican,* May 5, 1829; son's name: *ibid.* Subsequent relation of Davies to Berrien: see receipt of John Macpherson Berrien for $300 from the State of Georgia, May 13, 1822, University of Georgia MS, Telemon Cuyler Collection, and Berrien to Troup, May 7, 1826, *ibid.,* both cited with the permission of the University of Georgia.

Appeal. March — May 1821

"The number remaining in the hands of the Marshal . . ." Habersham to Adams, March 12, 1821, Department of State, *Miscellany Letters.*

Counsel at Milledgeville: Circ. Ct. Diary, May 8, 1821.

Johnson's biography: Donald Morgan, *Justice William Johnson* (Columbia, S.C., 1954), pp. 18-23; 41-51; his appearance: Charles Warren, *The Supreme Court in United States History* I, 468.

Reasoning and holdings of Justice Johnson: Opinion, Cir. Ct., May 11, 1821.

"a vice-consul, duly recognized . . ." *The Bello Corrunes* 6 Wheaton 151, 167 (1821).

Judge Bridlegoose: François Rabelais, *Des Faits et dicts héroiques du bon Pantagruel,* Book III, ch. 39, *Oeuvres,* ed. Ch. Marty-Laveaux (1870) vol. 187; trans. Thomas Urquhart, *The Tudor Translations,* ed. W.E. Henley, XXV, 202. "marvellously long-continued success . . ." Rabelais III, ch. 44.

Execution. July 1821

The lot in Savannah and the winners: Clerk's Report, Cir. Ct., July 16, 1821.

"I have deemed it not advisable . . ." Habersham to Adams, July 22, 1821, Department of State, *Miscellany Letters.*

Compensation. December 1821 — January 1822

"the residue of the Africans" and their division: Decree, Cir. Ct., December 28, 1821.

Cuyler's biography: Maud Churchill Nicoll, *The Earliest Cuylers in Holland and America and Some of Their Descendants* (New York, 1912), pp. 30, 38; Charlton as Grand Master: *The Republican,* December 7, 1821; Cuyler as Grand Master: *The Republican,* April 6, 1825.

Sale of the *Antelope* and division of proceeds: "Petition of Richard H. Wilde," *Reports . . . to the House of Representatives,* H. Rep. Doc. no. 56, 20th Cong., 1st Sess. (1827), p. 7.

"Notwithstanding however that in these cases . . ." Habersham to Adams, January 8, 1822, Department of State, *Miscellany Letters.*

5. If He Was a Man that Could Turn a State or Perhaps Even a County . . ."

Le Jeune Eugénie. September — December 1821

"ought to know . . ." R.F. Stockton to Daniel Webster, November 5, 1821, Daniel Webster, *Writings and Speeches* ed. James W. McIntyre (1900) XV, 208.

"against capturing vessels . . ." Adams to Daniel Brent (Adams' executive assistant) September 6, 1821, Adams, *Letterbook (Adams Papers MS,* Massachusetts Historical Society); cf. Adams to Brent, September 19, 182, *ibid.* The President's response: Monroe to Brent, September 15, 1821, Monroe VI, 193. For the later orders, see General Instructions and the Additional Instructions of the Navy Department, January 22, 1823, transmitted by Secretary of the Navy Thompson to Commodore Porter, Historical Society of Pennsylvania, Miscellany MS.

"You have certainly taken the safe side . . ." Wirt to Monroe, September 21, 1821, Library of Congress MS, Monroe Papers.

"I am satisfied . . ." Adams to Brent, September 22, 1821, Adams, *Letterbook.*

Cabinet discussion of *La Jeune Eugénie:* Adams V, 380-381, November 3, 1821.

Conversation with Wirt: Adams V, 387-388, November 6, 1821.

"the flag must be considered . . ." Adams V, 389-390, November 8, 1821.

"to the wishes . . ." *United States v. La Jeune Eugénie,* 26 *Federal Cases* 832 at 840; "they would conceal . . ." *idem.* at 841.

"like lumber . . . the utmost disorder . . . steeped to their mouths . . ." Joseph Story, Charge to the Grand Jury, Portland, Maine, *Miscellaneous Writings,* pp. 122-147. For partial texts of his charge to the other grand juries, substantially identical with the Portland charge, see W.W. Story, *Life and Letters of Joseph Story* (1850) I.

"incurably unjust and inhuman . . ." *U.S. v. La Jeune Eugénie,* 26 *Federal Cases* 832 at 847; "at a late period . . ." *idem.* at 850.

Postponement. February — March 1822

Privateer cases decided in 1822 and reported in 7 Wheaton: *The Gran Para,* p. 72; *The Monte Allegre,* and *The Rainha de los Anjos,* p. 520; *The Santissima Tinidad* and *The St. André,* p. 283; *The Arrogante Barcelones,* p. 496.

Antelope postponed: *The United States, Claimant of Sundry Negroes v. Charles Mulvey, Vice Consul,* and *United States v. Claimants of African Negroes Part of the Cargo of the Antelope or Ramirez,* Minutes of the United States Supreme Court, February Term, 1822. The case of the Vice Consul of Portugal and the case of the Vice Consul of Spain are thus treated as two separate cases, although they were merged for the purposes of argument and decision.

"if many members from these states . . ." Monroe to Spencer Roane, February 14, 1820, New York Public Library MS, Monroe Collection, quoted with permission of the Library.

"In respect to the candidates . . ." Story to Jeremiah Mason, February 21, 1822, George S. Holland, *Memoir, Autobiography and Correspondence of Jeremiah Mason* (1917), p. 256.

Number of Africans on *La Pensée:* Secretary of the Navy Thompson to Joseph Hemphill, Chairman of the Committee on the Slave Trade, February 7, 1821, p. 5, in Report of the Committee, H.R. Rep. No. 92, *House Reports,* 17 Cong., 1st Sess.

"The vessel with her cargo . . . the only difficulty . . ." Wirt to Monroe, January 22, 1822, *Official Opinions of the Attorneys General* I, 524-535.

Wirt's apoplexy: Joseph Story to Sarah Story, February 10, 1822, Story, *Life and Letters* I, 412.

Morel Accused. December 1821— October 1822

"as wary as a Jesuit . . ." Adams IV, 416, August 4, 1819.

Discussion of Morel: Adams V, 455, December 18, 1821.

Cuthbert and Tatnall recommend: Adams VI, 87, October 26, 1822; Tatnall's relation to Berrien, McCrary, *John Macpherson Berrien,* p. 113.

"the ineffaceable stain of blood . . ." Adams VI, 87, October 26, 1822.

"the Marshal for the District of Georgia . . ." and the ensuing discussion: Adams 86-87, October 26, 1822. Italics in original.

"at pleasure": An Act to Establish the Judicial Courts of the United States, September 24, 1789, *United States Statutes at Large* I, 87.

Payment to Habersham: "A Detailed Statement of the Sum Appropriated by the 7th Section of the Act, passed the 3rd of March, 1819, in addition to the Acts prohibiting the Slave Trade," 20th Congress, 1st Session, *Senate Document* No. 3, p. 10.

Morel was paid nothing further: *idem;* Morel's bill: Clerk's Report, *The Antelope,* December Term, 1826.

The Balance of the Attorney General.
September 1822 — February 1823

Man more conjugal than political: Aristotle, *Nichomachean Ethics,* p. 1719.

"appeared to think more about his salary . . ." Adams IV, 82, April 28, 1818.

"a very empty thing, stomachically speaking . . ." Wirt to Dabney Carr, February 13, 1813, reproduced in John P. Kennedy, *Life of William Wirt,* 91.

Wirt's liver: Wirt to John Clarke, May 28, 1822, William Wirt, *Letterbook* (Library of Congress MS); debts: Wirt to John White, May 1, 1822, *ibid.* "trial fees . . ." Wirt to his wife, April 17, 1822, Maryland Historical Society MS, Wirt Papers; "Only suppose it! . . ." Wirt to his wife, May 30, 1822, Wirt Papers, both quoted with the permission of the Society. Wirt's standard fee: Wirt to Thomas Carbury, April 13, 1823, *Letterbook;* ten children: Frances Norton Mason, *My Dearest Polly: Letters of Chief Justice Marshall to His Wife, with Their Background Political and Domestic, 1779 — 1831* (1967, p. 263. Wirt's salary: "An Act to increase the salaries of certain officers of government," February 20, 1819, *Public Statutes at Large* III, 484. "to prosecute . . ." An Act to establish the Judicial Courts of the United States, September 24, 1789, *idem,* I, 43.

"I see no difference . . ." Wirt to Monroe, September 27, 1822, *Opinions of the Attorneys General* I, 570.

"Virginia *autocracy* against slaves . . ." Adams VI, 71, October 1, 1822.

Foreign policy considerations: see Arthur F. Corwin, *Spain and the Abolition of Slavery in Cuba, 1817 — 1866 (1967),* pp. 35-46; Bethell, *The Abolition of the Brazilian Slave Trade* (1970), pp. 27-55.

"The great business in Washington . . ." Story to Nathaniel Williams, February 28, 1823, W.W. Story, *Life and Letters* I, 424.

"should, if possible, be decided . . ." Adams to Wirt, February 7, 1823, Department of State, *Domestic Letters* XX."This statute . . ." Adams to Canning, March 31, 1823, *American State Papers, Foreign Relations* V, 329.

Bates, the anti-slave trade collector: Elizabeth Walker to Story, January 15, 1821, Michigan University MS, microfilm, Joseph Story Collections.

130 settlers: American Society for Colonizing, *Sixth Annual Report* (1823), p. 12; 7 children kidnapped, 7 men killed: Jehudi Ashmun to Secretary Thompson, November 26, 1822, printed in American Society, *Seventh Annual Report* (1824), p. 50, and Ashmun to Thompson, December 7, 1822, *ibid.,* 51.

"there is much jealousy . . ." E. Ayres to Secretary Thompson, June 18, 1823, printed in *Report of the Secretary of the Navy to the President,* December 1, 1823, *House Doc.* No. 2, 18th Cong., 1st Sess. (1823).

Wirt's private cases in the Supreme Court in 1823: reported in 8 Wheaton: *Wormly v. Wormly,* p. 421 (purchase of land); *Corporation of Washington v. Pratt,* p. 681 (tax matter for Washington Surveyor's case); *Nichols v. Anderson,* p. 365.

"Continued": Docket of the Supreme Court, February Term, 1823.

The Case Abandoned. February — April 1824

Wirt's private cases in the Supreme Court in 1824, reported in 9 Wheaton: *Mason v. Muncaster,* p. 445 (Episcopal glebe lands); *Dodridge v. Thompson,* p. 469 (land case); *Kirk v. Smith,* p. 241 (land case); *Taylor v. Mason,* p. 325 (trust case); *The Monte Allegre,* 616 (tobacco purchase).

Doubt as to Crawford's ability to write his name: Wirt to Monroe, July 15, 1824, *Opinions of the Attorneys General* I, 670-674.

Adams' ambition as barrier: Stratford Canning to George Canning, June 6, 1823, *Public Record Office, Foreign Office* Series 5, vol. 176.

"Piracy . . . the nature of the crime . . ." Adams to Canning, June 24, 1823, *American State Papers, Foreign Relations,* 5, 332.

Convention of March 13, 1824; *idem.,* pp. 320.

Payment "in full": Clerk's Report, Cir. Ct., 1827, reproduced in Wilde, *Petition . . .,* House Doc. No. 56, 20th Cong., 1st Sess., 1828, p. 7. Mulvey's death: obituary, *The Republican,* March 18, 1823.

Wirt's decision to abandon the case; Berrien to Governor Troup of Georgia, June 28, 1825, reproduced in *The Republican,* September 22, 1825.

The Case Resurrected. May 1824 — February 1825

Senate vote on Convention: *Senate Executive Journal,* pp. 3, 385, May 22, 1824. On the whole episode: Samuel Flagg Bemis, *John Quincy Adams and the Foundations of American Foreign Policy* (1949), pp. 430-435.

Berrien's belief as to role of member of Colonization Society: Berrien to Troup, June 28, 1825, reproduced in *The Republican,* September 22, 1825.

Promulgation of laws for Liberia: American Society for Colonization, *Constitution, Government and Digest of the Laws of Liberia* (Washington, 1825), p. 3. 380 colonists: *Niles Weekly Register* XXVIII, 34, March 19, 1825.

"felt presence was my strength . . ." Francis Scott Key, "Efficacy of Prayer," printed in Delaplaine, *Francis Scott Key,* p. 247. On his activity on behalf of the Episcopal Church: *ibid.,* pp. 244-246; death of son: *ibid.*, p. 222; "servant of God . . . slave of the world": *ibid.*, p. 228; Charlton as cousin: *ibid.*, p. 232.

"But Sir as to Mr. Charlton . . ." Key to Charlton, 1824, "Letters of Francis Scott Key," *Maryland Historical Magazine* XLIV, 288; reprinted in Delaplaine, *Francis Scott Key.*

On the War of the Giants, see Harry Ammon, *James Monroe; The Quest for National Identity* (1971), p. 493.

"kindling into fury": Adams VI, 491, February 3, 1825.

"the bitterest Federalist in Heart & Soul . . ." Harris to General Mitchell, September 4, 1824, University of Georgia MS, Keith Reid Collection, quoted with permission of the University.

Sentiments of Maryland's congressional delegation: William Plumer, Jr. to William Plumer, January 4, 1825, *The Missouri Compromise and Presidential Politics, 1820 — 1825,* ed. Everett Somerville Brown (1926), p. 126. Wooing of delegation: Adams VI, 492, February 3, 1825; Adams VI, 499-500, February 7, 1825.

McKim's subscription of $500: American Society, *Second Annual Report* (1819), p. 122. The reduction of his subscription: *Fifth Annual Report* (1822), p. 111.

McKim's visits to Adams: Adams VI, 468, January 15, 1825; Adams VI, 473, 475, January 21, 1825. ("J. McKim" is given for "I. McKim" at 473.)

Maryland goes by one vote: William Plumer, Jr., to William Plumer, February 13, 1825, Brown, ed., *The Missouri Compromise,* p. 135. Clay's appointment, Adams VI, 505, February 10, 1825.

Meeting in the Supreme Court Room: American Society for Colonizing, *Eighth Annual Report* (1825), p. 3. Addresses of Lieutenant Stockton and Reverend Gurley: "Annual Meeting of the Colonization Society," *The African Repository and Colonial Journal* I, 13-15, 18.

Dates of argument: Minutes of the Supreme Court, February Term, 1825.

6. Supreme Law

An Uncommon Excitement. February 26 — March 3, 1825

Dates of argument and appearances of counsel: United States Supreme Court, Minutes, February Term, 1825. (The Minutes are not in agreement with the printed dates in 10 Wheaton and appear more reliable.)

Key's Supreme Court cases involving slavery: *Wood v. Davis* 7 Cranch 271 (1812); *Negress Sally Henry v. Ball* 1 Wheaton 1 (1816); *Negro John Davis v. Wood* 1 Wheaton 5 (1816); *Scott v. Negro Ben* 6 Cranch 1 (1810); *Mima Queen and Child v. Hepburn* 7 Cranch 290 (1812); (also *Gettings v. Burch's Administratrix* 9 Cranch 372 (1815) (a suit between slave-owners).

Wirt's cases on ship forfeitures: *La Josefa Segunda* 5 Wheaton 338 (1820); *La Concepcion* 6 Wheaton 235 (1821); *The Bello Corrunes* 6 Wheaton 151 (1821); *The Mary Ann* 8 Wheaton 378 (1823); *The St. Iago de Cuba* 9 Wheaton 409 (1824); *The Merino* 9 Wheaton 391 (1824).

Berrien's election: *Niles Weekly Register* XXVII, 192, November 20, 1824. Berrien's 1818 Supreme Court cases, all in 3 Wheaton: *The Diana,* 58; *The Atlanta,* 409, *Murray v. Baker,* 541.

Ingersoll's background: "Ingersoll, Charles Jared," *Dictionary of National Biography* IX, 465-467. Ingersoll's privateer cases: *The Estrella* 4 Wheaton 297 (1819); *The Josefa Segunda* 5 Wheaton 338 (1820); *La Amistad de Rues* 5 Wheaton 385 (1820); *The Merino* 9 Wheaton 391 (1824). "a monstrous fool . . ." G.M. Dallas to B.C. Howard, October 21, 1817, Maryland Historical Society MS, B.C. Howard Papers, quoted with the permission of the Historical Society.

"certainly have the advantage . . ." Berrien to Harris, March 4, 1825, New York Public Library Misc. MS, quoted with the permission of the Library.

"worthy of all praise": *Niles Weekly Register* XXVIII, 49, March 26, 1825.

"enlisted in a splendid manner . . . closed with a thrilling and even electrifying . . ." Henry Stuart Foote, *A Casket of Reminiscences* (1874), p. 13.

Argument in *The Antelope:* Quotations are not from a verbatim record of the speeches, but from the summary and paraphrase of the argument by Henry Wheaton, *The Antelope* 10 Wheaton 66 at 70-114. "Our national policy . . ." 71; "those human beings . . ." 71-72 (italics in original); "consisted merely . . . Slaves are . . ." 78-79; the lot unsatisfactory: 81; Jackson unauthorized: 82; the "subjects of Spain . . ." 85; "[W]ould it become the United States . . ." 89; *La Jeune Eugénie* criticized: 92-97; presumption of slavery: 100; "body of political ethics . . ." 101; "to anticipate, by judicial legislation . . ." 105; the Africans are "parties to the cause . . ." 106; the *Dallas* authorized: 107; "The Africans stand before the court . . ." 108 (italics in original); "no excuse or palliation . . ." 111; the Africans are free persons: 114. *Somerset's Case: Somerset v. Stewart* 98, English Reports 499 (King's Bench, 1772).

Judgment Day. March 16, 1825

Story's background: Gerald T. Dunne, *Joseph Story and the Rise of the Supreme Court* (New York, 1970), pp. 26-76. "I dare say you will think . . ." Story to Washington, December 21, 1821, Washington State Historical Society MS, quoted with the permission of the Society.

"he thinks I am right . . ." Story to Jeremiah Mason, February 21, 1822, in George S. Holland, *Memoir and Correspondence of Jeremiah Mason* (1911), p. 256.

Marshall's special trip for Colonization Society meeting and his role in the Richmond — Manchester Auxiliary: Frances Norton Mason, *My Dearest Polly: Letters of John Marshall to His Wife* (1967), pp. 252, 256. His election as National Vice-President, American Society for Colonizing, *Eighth Annual Report* (1825), p. 3.

"However the feelings . . . a right to property . . ." *Mima Queen and Child v. Hepburn* 7 Cranch 290 at 295 (1812).

"You may look back with pleasure . . ." Marshall to Monroe, December 13, 1824, printed in John Edwards Usher, *The Political and Economic Doctrines of John Marshall* (1914), p. 180.

"deeply and earnestly . . ." Story to Daniel Webster, August 6, 1822, W.W. Story, *Life and Letters* I, 421.

The sale of Bushrod Washington's slaves: "Judge Washington and his Slaves," *Niles Weekly Register* XXI, 1, September 1, 1821. "any person questioning our right . . ." Washington to the Editor of the *Federal Republican* (Baltimore), reprinted *Niles Weekly Register* XXI, 70-71, September 29, 1821 (italics in original).

Duvall's background: Irving Dillard, "Gabriel Duvall," *The Justices of the United States Supreme Court, 1789 — 1969,* ed. Leon Friedman and Fred L. Israel (1969), pp. 419-424; and Dillard, "Duvall, Gabriel," *Dictionary of American Biography* XXI (Supplement One), 272-274. His writing record: Donald G. Morgan, *Justice William Johnson* (1954), pp. 306-307. "the Shorters . . ." *Wood v. Davis* 7 Cranch 271 (1812). "People of color . . . It will be universally admitted . . ." *Mima Queen and Child v. Hepburn* 7 Cranch 290 at 298-299.

Thompson's background: Gerald T. Dunne, "Smith Thompson," *The Justices of the United States Supreme Court* I, 479-480, 484-485. His position on the Missouri bill: Adams V, 9, March 2, 1820; his opposition to Adams on *La Jeune Eugénie:* Adams V, 380 and 389, November 3 and 8, 1821. "more formidable to human liberty . . ." Adams IV, 354, April 29, 1819.

"This would seem to be doing business . . ." *Niles Weekly Register* XXVIII, 49 (March 26, 1825).

A dozen more to be decided: United States Supreme Court, Minutes, February Term, 1825.

DeWolfe's Kentucky case: *DeWolfe v. Johnson* 10 Wheaton 367 (1825). Clay as DeWolfe's lawyer, DeWolfe to Clay, January 3, 1821, *The Papers of Henry Clay,* ed. James F. Hopkins, III, 3. Clay's correspondence shows DeWolfe visiting Cuba in 1821 (*ibid.,* III, 453), but fails to show DeWolfe in direct contact with Cuesta Manzanal and Brother.

"most important judgment . . ." W.W. Story, *Life and Letters of Joseph Story* I, 481.

The Plattsburgh: 10 Wheaton 133; *The Josefa Segunda:* 10 Wheaton 313 (1825).

Marshall's opinions in the 1825 Term, reported in 10 Wheaton: *Wayman v. Southard,* 20-50 (federal practice); *The Antelope,* 113-132; *Elmendorf v. Taylor,* 156-181 (Kentucky land case); *Carneal v. Banks,* 181-190 (Kentucky land case); *The Dos Hermanos,* 309-311 (War of 1812 prize case); *Brent v. Davis,* 395-404 ("the National"); *Corporation of Washington v. Young,* 406-410 ("the National"); *Day v. Chism,* 448-454 (Tennessee land case); *McDowell v. Peyton,* 455-464 (Kentucky land case); *The Palmyra,* 503-504 (ship forfeiture for piracy). On the Washington Lottery as "the National," see *Niles Weekly Register* XXVII, 148.

Marshall's opinion on the slave trade's status: *The Antelope* 10 Wheaton 66, 114-121.

The Proof of Ownership

Marshall on the Spanish and Portuguese claims: 10 Wheaton 66 at 123-131.

The Vote

"very able": "Judge Marshall's Opinion," *The African Repository and Colonial Journal* I, 353, February 1826.

The Lottery

"The individuals must be designated . . ." Africans "which were brought in" and "which may be . . . the said decree is . . . affirmed": Marshall, in *The Antelope,* 10 Wheaton at 128-133.

7. Sam, Lucy, Joe . . . and Boatswain

The Embarrassment of Counsel. June —July 1825

"the law in Somerset's Case . . ." Governor Troup, Message, June 7, 1825. Secessionist spirit in Georgia over federal handling of the Creek Indians: Adams VII, 3-6.

Berrien absent when Wirt spoke: Berrien to Joseph Henry Lumpkin, May 31, 1825, University of Georgia MS, Telemon Cuyler Collection, quoted with the permission of the University of Georgia.

Wirt wrote each Justice: Wirt to William Johnson, July 22, 1825, Maryland Historical Society MS, Wirt Papers, quoted with the permission of the Historical Society.

"nor can I imagine . . ." Washington to Wirt, July 9, 1825, University of Virginia, Washington Family Papers, quoted with the permission of the University of Virginia.

Impasse. December 1825 — March 1826

One to one split: *The Antelope,* 11 Wheaton 413-414 (1827).

Morel's nomination by Adams: *Senate Executive Journal,* pp. 3, 449.

"if some few citizens . . ." Adams, First Annual Message, *Messages and Addresses of the Presidents of the United States,* ed. Edwin Williams (1846) I.

"125 to 130 . . . to be sent to agency . . ." Samuel L. Southard, *Annual Report of the Secretary of the Navy, with the President's Message Showing the Operation of that Department in 1825,* American State Papers, Naval Affairs, II, no. 268, p. 100.

"It will be your duty . . ." Southard to John W. Peaco, December 28, 1925, *Annual Report of the Secretary of the Navy, Showing the Condition of the Navy in the Year 1826,* American State Papers, Naval Affairs, II, no. 319, pp. 749-750.

Marshall's New Year's Day letter, described in Southard's reply, January 5, 1826, *ibid.,* p. 750. "created surprise . . ." Southard to Habersham, January 3, 1826 *ibid.,* p. 750.

"the mode of designating . . ." *The Antelope* 11 Wheaton 414 (1826).

Designation. May — December 1826

"designate by proof . . ." Cir. Ct., Decree, May 9, 1826.

Total Africans taken off the *Columbia: The Antelope* 10 Wheaton at 132-133.

"It is extremely desirable . . ." Southard to Habersham, August 10, 1826, *Annual Report of the Secretary of the Navy . . . 1826,* American State Papers, Naval Affairs, II, no. 319, p. 751.

The Marshal's bill: George Glen, Register, Cir. Ct., *Report,* November Term, 1826.

1826 Opinion of Johnson: *The Antelope,* Cir. Ct., December 1, 1826.

$20,286.98 to Marshal Morel: "A Detailed Statement of the Sum Appropriated by the Seventh Section of the Act, passed the 3rd of March, 1819, in addition to the Acts prohibiting the Slave Trade," *Senate Document* No. 3, 20th Congress, 1st Sess., p. 7. Removal of Africans from Marshal: Report of George Glen, Register, Cir. Ct., November Term 1826. Rejection of Marshal's bill for $12,659: "Statement Showing the Expenditure of the Appropriation for the Prohibition of the Slave Trade During the Year 1826 and Estimate for 1827," *House Document* no. 69, 19th Congress, 2nd Sess., p. 3.

One to one split: *The Antelope* 12 Wheaton 546 at 548 (1827).

Testimony of Richardson, Morel, Haupt, Berthelot: Cir. Ct., December 1, 1826.

"The Negroes of the cargo . . ." Glen, Record, *Tne Antelope,* Cir. Ct., December 1, 1826. Names and possessors of Africans: *idem.*

"the primest . . ." Morel, Testimony, Cir. Ct., December 1, 1826.

The Third Appeal. January — March 1827

Wirt's attendance scheduled: He is reported as arguing the case in 12 Wheaton 456; this error is not found in the Minutes. "I told him I could not . . ." Adams VI, 235, March 6, 1827. "would be necessarily engaged . . ." Adams VII, 237, March 12, 1827; the case was *United States v. Gooding.* "I am *obliged* I find to be at the President's . . ." Wirt to Swanson [undated], Maryland Historical Society MS, quoted with the permission of the Society.

"there is no credible . . ." Justice Trimble restating counsel's argument in *The Antelope* 12 Wheaton 545 at 552 (1827).

Ogden v. Saunders: 12 Wheaton 213. The big case of 1827: see Dunne, *Joseph Story,* pp. 261-265. An idea worthy only of Africa: Justice Johnson in *Ogden v. Saunders* 12 Wheaton 213 at 184; *"Summum ius . . ." ibid.* at 283.

Trimble's background: Fred L. Israel, "Robert Trimble" in *The Justices of the United States Supreme Court, 1789 — 1969,* ed. Leon Friedman and Fred L. Israel (1969), 513-518. Wickliffe's recommendation of Trimble: Wickliffe to Clay, March 7, 1826, University of Kentucky, microfilm 2:6-990, Clay Papers. Trimble's switch from Crawford: Robert Trimble to David Trimble, August 13, 1827, microfilm 3:11-1911, Clay Papers. His vote for Adams: *The Papers of Henry Clay,*

IV. Berrien's opposition: *Senate Executive Journal,* p. 3, 538, May 9, 1826.

Trimble opinion: *The Antelope* 12 Wheaton 550-554.

8. The Interest and Humanity of Congressman Wilde

Transportation. June — August 1827

"and now remains at a charge . . ." Adams VII, 284-285, June 2, 1827.

Todson's background: Adams VII, 209-212; *Register of Officers . . . on September 30, 1825,* p. 76. "believed that it was no idle menace . . . I am in the hands . . ." Adams VII: 192-193, November 29, 1826. Adams remitted the fine: Adams VII, 239, March 15, 1827; meeting with Todson: Adams VII, 282-283, May 30, 1827. "had originated in the badness . . ." Adams VII, 285, June 2. "extremely anxious . . ." Adams VII, 287-288, June 4. Southard appoints Todson: Adams VII, 292, June 12. His salary and title: "A Statement of expenditures under the appropriation for the prohibition of the Slave Trade since the 1st of December 1827," *House Doc. No. 2,* 20th Congress, 2nd Session, pp. 127-128. Todson's earlier salary: *Register of Officers,* p. 94.

"a number of negroes . . ." Adams VII, 285, June 2, 1827.

$335 for Marshal Morel: "A Detailed Statement of the Sum Appropriated . . . in addition to the Acts prohibiting the Slave Trade," *Senate Document* No. 3, 20th Congress, 1st Sess., p. 10-8; Number of Africans from the *Antelope* put aboard the *Norfolk:* The most reliable record appears to be the bill paid by the Navy to the owners of the *Norfolk* for transportation. The owners had no reason to understate the number transported. The bill is for 129 grown persons and for 14 persons under the age of ten, "A statement of expenditure . . . since the 1st of December 1827," *House Doc.* No. 2, 20th Congress, 2nd Session, pp. 127-218. From this total of 143, there must be subtracted 12 who were freed Africans from New Orleans and were also transported on the *Norfolk:* "A Detailed Statement . . . the Slave Trade," *Sen. Doc.* No. 3, 20th Cong., 1st Sess., p. 10-8. No more than 131 Africans were billed as from Savannah. It seems reasonable to suppose that a dozen of the 14 under the age of ten were Savannah Africans.

Arrival of *Norfolk,* 3 deaths and 2 births aboard: Todson to Secretary Southard, August 29, 1827, *Appendix to Annual Report of the Secretary of the Navy, American State Papers, Naval Affairs* III, 60. The dumb, the idiot, and the invalids: Todson, "Statement of the disposition made, and actual situation (September 14th) of the 142 recaptured Africans received at the Agency for recaptured Africans, Cape Mesurado," *H.R. Rept. No. 348, 20th Congress, 1st Sess. (1828) p. 298.*

Liberation. August — December 1827

"all persons . . ." *Constitution, Government and Digest of the Laws of Liberia as confirmed and established by the Boards of Managers of the American Colonization Society May 23, 1825.*

"five spacious apartments . . ." Ashmun, Schedule of United States property attached to the Agency for Recaptured Africans, Cape Mesurado, September 1, 1827, printed for the Committee to whom were referred the memorial of the American Society for Colonizing . . . *H.R. Rep.* No. 348, 21st Cong., 1st Sess. (1830), pp. 285-287.

"the terms on which the recaptured Africans . . ." Todson to Secretary Southard, August 29, 1827, Appendix D to Annual Report of the Secretary of the Navy, *American State Papers, Naval Affairs* III, 61. "shall not prove them unworthy . . ." Ashmun to Secretary Southard, August 28, 1827, printed in *H.R. Rep.* No. 348, 21st Cong., 1st Sess., (1830), p. 281. Employment of Africans: Todson, "Statement of the disposition made . . ." *ibid.*, pp. 289-291.

One African eaten; one child dies: Ashmun to Secretary Southard, December 22, 1827, printed in *H.R. Rep.* No. 348, 21st Cong., 1st Sess. (1830), p. 284.

"These people have proved . . ." *ibid.*, p. 284.

Christmas in Savannah. December 1827

Printed as an appendix to Richard H. Wilde, *Petition to the Senate and House of Representatives of the United States,* November 30, 1827, *House Doc.* No. 56, 20th Cong., 1st Sess. (1828), are the following: Order of Judge Cuyler, December 1, 1827, taxing the court costs, Marshal's charge, salvage, and proctors' fees; Report of Glen, Clerk, Cir. Ct., November Term 1827, giving the salvage owing Jackson and the valuation of the Africans; receipt from Berrien to Gaston, "attorney in fact" for Cuesta Manzanal and Brother, November 17, 1827, for $1950; receipt from Morel to Wilde, December 26, 1827, for $6347; receipt from Morel, as Harris' executor, to Wilde, December 26, 1827, for $500; receipt from Charlton to Gaston, "attorney for Cuesta Manzanal and Brother," for $500 paid by Wilde, undated. The amount allegedly paid the owner is given by Senator Berrien in the Senate, December 31, 1827, Gales and Seaton, *Register of Debates in Congress,* 20th Cong., 1st Sess., IV, 30.

37 Africans: Act of May 2, 1828, 20th Cong., 1st Sess., *Public Statutes at Large* VI, 376, gives the bond at $14,800 — which, divided by $400, yields 37.

$3,750 to Berrien: "A Detailed Statement of the Sum Appropriated . . . in Addition to the Act prohibiting the Slave Trade," *Senate Doc.* No. 3, 20th Congress, 1st Session (1828), p. 10-8; $400 to Jackson: *ibid.*, p. 8; $1350 to Berrien: "A statement of expenditures under the appropriation . . . since the 1st of December 1827," *House Doc.* No. 2, 20th Cong., 2nd Sess., p. 127.

Condemnation of the *Dallas* and Jackson's discharge: Adams VI, 401, July 21, 1824.

Acceptance of Habersham's resignation: Clay to Habersham, April 27, 1827, State Dept., *Domestic Letters.* "competent member . . . You no doubt possess . . ." Clay to Johnson, April 27, 1827, *ibid.*

Nomination of new District Attorney: *Senate Executive Journal,* pp. 3, 579; confirmation, December 24, 1827: *ibid.*, pp. 3, 513.

Sunbeams from Cucumbers. December 1827

Wilde's biography: Edward Llewellyn Tucker, *Richard Henry Wilde: Life and Selected Poems* (doctoral dissertation, University of Georgia, 1957; microfilmed, University Microfilms, Ann Arbor, Michigan) 3; his birth order; *ibid.*, 6; early life, 6-17; early political career: 21-27; later political career: 50-51, 88-100; "with an expansive forehead . . ." Charles Colcock Jones, Jr., a contemporary, quoted in *ibid.*, 49; close friendship with Clay: 83; with Sumner: 119; career in New Orleans: 146-147; title from Fiescole: 121; Italian sojourn: 109-191; income from Florida plantation: 127. See also Knight, *Reminiscenses of Famous Georgians,* pp. 147-155; Barbara Wilkinson Jenkins, *Richard Henry Wilde: Some Notes on His Life* (typewritten M.A. thesis, University of Georgia, 1938), pp. 32-34. Wilde's role in the Troup controversy: Berrien to Wilde, June 20, 1825, and Wilde to Berrien, June 25, 1825, University of Georgia MS, Telemon Cuyler Collection; Wilde as referee of Berrien's fee: Berrien to Troup, May 7, 1826, *idem.* "Sorrell's deliverance . . ." Berrien to Wilde, December 30, 1826, Library of Congress MS, Berrien's Correspondence, quoted with the permission of the Library of Congress. Wilde a frequent visitor of Berrien: McCrary, *John Macpherson Berrien,* p. 125.

"While I was in Savannah . . ." Wilde to Berrien, May 22, 1827, University of North Carolina MS (Berrien Collection), quoted with the permission of the University of North Carolina. "My plan is simply this . . ." *idem.*

"of the repugnance of these people . . ." Wilde, "Petition to the United States Senate . . ." *H.R. Doc.* No. 56, 20th Cong., 1st Sess. (1828), pp. 3-4.

"humane proceedings . . ." Board of Managers, American Colonization Society, Resolution, December 12, 1827, printed in Wilde, "Petition," p. 8.

Law as Berrien associate: John Macpherson Berrien, Receipt to State of Georgia, May 13, 1822, University of Georgia MS, Telemon Cuyler Collection. Morel as executor: Clerk's Report, November 1827.

Wilde's Petition dated November 30, 1827, in the Senate, referred to Judiciary Committee December 17 and reported December 20: Wilde, "Petition," p. 1

"from motives of humanity . . ." Gales and Seaton, IV, 30.

American Enslavement. January — May 1828

Wilde's petition in the House: "these unfortunate creatures . . . in the pure kindness . . ." *ibid.,* p. 915. Debate on Wilde petition: *ibid.,* pp. 915, 957-966.

Motion to pay Wilde, and the vote, April 25, 1828: *ibid.,* pp. 2501-2503. Text of the law: Act of May 2, 1828, 20th Cong., 1st Sess., chapter 43, *Public Statutes at Large* VI, 376.

Disposition of slaves of Wilde, *The Mercury,* September 10, 1828.

Sale of Albemarle slaves: Monroe to James Madison, March 28, 1828, Monroe VII, 164.

9. Retrospect

"his most attractive characteristic," McCrary, *John Macpherson Berrien,* p. 406.

"the most exciting and encouraging . . ." L. C. Tuthill, *Success in Life — The Lawyer* (1850), Preface. "the very *beau ideal* . . ." Samuel L. Southard, *Discourse on the Professional Character and Virtues of the Late William Wirt* (1834), p. 47.

"the Department's Greatest Secretary," Graham H. Stuart, *The Department of State. A History of Its Organization, Procedure, and Personnel* (1949) 52.

"our great superiority . . ." Adams to Ingersoll, June 19, 1823, *Writings,* ed. Ford, VII, 488.

"Judicial objectivity . . ." Donald M. Roper, "In Quest of Judicial Objectivity: The Marshall Court and the Legitimation of Slavery," *Stanford*

Law Review, (1969) XXI, 534. "had little alternative . . ." Kent Newmyer, "On Assessing the Court in History," *ibid.,* p. 542. "the moral issue . . ." Charles Warren, *The Supreme Court in United States History* (1928) I, 585.

"consistently strove . . ." Donald G. Morgan, *Justice William Johnson* (1954) p. 137.

"no man could bestow . . ." Story, "Robert Trimble," *Miscellaneous Writings,* p. 802. Story is quoted in Israel, "Robert Trimble," *The Justices of the United States Supreme Court* I, 518. Trimble's opinion in *The Antelope* follows.

"When I consider his might . . ." Oliver Wendell Holmes, Jr., "Response of Chief Justice Holmes," in "John Marshall: The Tribute of Massachusetts," *John Marshall: Life, Character and Judicial Service,* comp. and ed. John F. Dillon (1903) I, 207.

"heartless sophistry . . . cold-blooded apathy . . ." Adams, *Argument in the Case of the United States v. Cinque* [*The Amistad*] (reprinted 1969) p. 16; "wedged in . . ." p. 110; "Is it possible . . .?" p. 82. In the phrase "thrilling regions of thick-ribbed ice," Adams adapted a line from Shakespeare's great play on retributive justice, *Measure for Measure* (III,i,123).

Index

Index

Index

Index

Index